Humor Consultant --------------------------------- Margery Eliscu

Journalism Advisor, Washington Bureau -------------- Bill Gold

World Series Producer (Gillette) ----------------------- Joel Nixon

Sportscaster Historian --------------------------------- Curt Smith

Photographic Credits ---------------------------- George Kalinsky
Bob Wolff Collection including
Washington Senator pictures
by Don Wingfield, and photos
by Norman Driscoll, Reni,
George Havens, Wallace Kammann,
Karas, Richard Collins,
John Maguire, Tore Heskestad,
David Mintzer, GFI Photo Reproductions,
NBC-TV, ABC-TV, CBS-TV,
Madison Square Garden Network,
Mutual Broadcasting System, and WTTG.

Publications Credits -------- Bob Wolff's New York-Cincinnati
telecast story, his Baltimore Colts -
New York Giants overtime
championship game account, and
his Joe Schaeffer article all appeared
in *The New York Times*. His
Don Larsen game story was printed
previously in Maury Allen's
Voices of Sports book. His Harmon Killebrew
softball story appeared previously in an
Ira Berkow column in *The New York Times*.
Rick Wolff's "Triumphant Return"
was in *Sports Illustrated*.

To Jane

Who, for the past 50 years, has not only pointed me in the right direction, but has also driven me there as well.

While watching Jane in action, I have taken voluminous notes on how to pack, read road maps, cook, clean, keep a checkbook, pay bills, shop, dress, motivate, encourage, edit, nurse, bind a family together, make friends everywhere, inspire love and affection from all, and epitomize all that a human being can be.

Having observed all this, I can truthfully say that, over the next 50 years, I should be a better-informed passenger.

BW

Chapter 1

"But First, a Word from the Sponsor"

When the sponsor writes against your name
What he wants to hear
It's not who won or lost the game
It's how you sold the beer.

I almost fell by the wayside during my early years of doing television play-by-play for the Washington Senators on WTTG in Washington.

"Old Georgetown" was the sponsoring beer. At the end of every inning, commercial announcer Johnny Batchelder would demonstrate on camera how thirst-quenching the beer was by downing half a glass or more. No problem. Except for those long, hot doubleheaders in the late August heat.

By the middle of the second game (and after a dozen or so beer commercials), John would be holding the glass of beer in one hand and gripping a rail for support with the other.

That's when I offered my advice to save the day and the sponsor.

"Get a bucket," I suggested. "Fake a swallow and when the

red light on the camera goes off, just spit the beer out. Why you'll even be good for extra innings that way." And so he tried it.

"Boy, that's great beer," exulted John, late in the game the next day. He then filled his mouth with a swig and held the explosion for the right moment.

But John beat the gun — came out of the blocks too soon. He was still on camera.

Viewers who had just heard his glowing endorsement of Old Georgetown now watched in amazement as Johnny spat a stream of amber suds into the bucket.

I don't remember who won the game, but I know we lost the sponsor. Those suds went right down the drain and took us with them.

By the time the National Brewing Company arrived on the scene, we had given up beer drinking on camera for beer pouring. I spent an entire month in spring training in Orlando, Florida, mastering the new art. A quick middle-of-the-glass pour, a surge of foam, the proper head — and no slopover.

It may sound funny now, but in those days such a skill was vital to one's success as a sportscaster.

When I came north, I had the touch — in fact, I could pour equally well with either hand.

Opening Day at Griffith Stadium in Washington. Half an hour before the first pitch. I was writing down lineups, checking game notes, and putting together my chart of who was who in the presidential party, when the advertising director of the brewing company suddenly appeared in the booth.

"Gentlemen," he said, "one last pour before the season begins. Let's make sure you have it right." He handed me a glass and a bottle of the sponsor's beer.

I stood, faced the camera, smiled, and began talking and

pouring simultaneously. Eyes straight ahead, sensing the tilt of the bottle, knowing through constant practice when the deed was done.

I then looked to check the result. I was standing in a pool of beer.

"Just rehearsal," I blurted, hiding my embarrassment. "Don't worry — I'll be ready when the game begins."

The game was great, but I got knocked out of the box in my first commercial pour. The beer cascaded over the side of the glass, forming a small foamy river as it streamed over my papers, my suit, and my shoes. What a mess.

My associate, Joe DiMona, saved me in the post-game sponsor's meeting. Joe worked with me in Washington while going to law school, before embarking on a successful writing career. Using his legal background, Joe made a telling argument for the defense.

"The beer Bob poured in spring training came out of a refrigerator, always at the same temperature. That's where Bob perfected the knack. The beer today was warm and stored in a hot press room. Bob's touch is excellent. He can do the job. What we need is a refrigerator in the booth."

My career continued in Washington. Next stop New York.

The New York Knicks were playing in the 69th Regiment Armory. The game was being televised on WPIX-TV, New York.

"When you start the game," I was instructed, "pause between each sponsor's name when you read the opening billboard. That gives the production assistant time to flip each visual card on the easel. After you mention Krueger Beer and say it has 'Zing,' the 'Zing' card will be shown on the TV screen."

That night two cards stuck together. "Krueger Beer has.....

Wildroot Cream Oil." Could have been a hair-raising experience, but the sponsors didn't laugh.

At Madison Square Garden, the facilities were first-rate. The sponsor was Robert Burns Cigars. I trained hard for my debut. Don Carney of WPIX gave me cigar-smoking lessons. "Here's how to hold it, here's how to stick the cigar in your mouth — for gosh sakes, look like a cigar smoker...."

The agency producer, Dave Berman, gave me the privilege of using my own words in the commercial. And there I was on camera, just me and the high-priced, glass-enclosed, highly heralded Robert Burns Imperial.

The words flowed. I felt in full command as I told the viewers about the cigar's fine, rich, moist tobacco, preserved so well.

As final proof, I even held the cigar under my nose, took an enchanted whiff, became enraptured with its wonderful aroma and concluded the commercial with my most satisfied smile.

The phone was already ringing when I stepped off the set. The first call was from the company's vice president. "The words were just great, but never before have I seen anyone sniff a cigar through the glass tube. Next time, would you please...."

Undaunted, my next stop was the ABC-TV network, hosting pre- and post-game football shows. Prince Albert came into my life — a pipe tobacco.

My job was to hold up the can, dip my hand in, let the moist tobacco sift through my fingers, and get ecstatic over its feel and quality.

Now I was on camera. I showed the audience the can — but then became horror-stricken when I found I couldn't get the lid off. Someone had clamped it tightly shut after my earlier rehearsal.

I kept tugging on the lid — live and coast-to-coast — smiling and mentioning the product's superior qualities as perspiration rolled down my cheeks. I then put the can under the table between my legs and kept yanking at the lid with my free arm.

Ten seconds left to go in the commercial. One final yank — too hard — lid and can finally parted — and I was covered with flying tobacco. The Prince abdicated that show at season's end.

Tobacco was later outlawed from the airwaves in the nicotime, one might say, but after my experiences with beer and tobacco, I was glad when I finally got a sponsor that seemed innocent enough. Vitalis took up the sponsorship and I was recruited to help wage war on those misguided souls who used "greasy kid stuff."

I got off to a good head start with Vitalis, I thought, but beginning with my second show on ABC-TV, I noticed a mysterious stranger who, unannounced, would come into the studio just before airtime and sit there staring intently at me.

After the fourth program, an emergency meeting was called, and "Mr. X" was right in the middle of it.

My hair was the big topic. My continuance on the show was in jeopardy. "Mr. X" stated that it looked as though I had on that much-despised "greasy kid stuff."

I swore my innocence, but to no avail. The next day was spent in testing everything on my hair from the sponsor's product on down. Even complete dryness didn't seem to work; the glare from my greaseless hair remained.

Finally, the director bellowed, "Let's lower the overhead lights and try it." I sat in the semi-darkness and waited for the decision.

A few minutes later the Vitalis man, still after my scalp, gave the final command: "Turn off the overheads altogether." Gone was any glint off my hair. I was now just a shadow of my former self, but my hair was now right for the part and the show went on. Saved again.

Looking back on it all today, there's no telling what might have happened next if technology had not come to my rescue with the invention of videotape.

The advent of videotape, of course, meant no more live commercials. No more crying over spilled beer, no more worrying about "greasy kid stuff," no more concern about my career going up in tobacco smoke. Now, if at first the commercial doesn't succeed, just tape again. And again.

Like I said, I was one of the fortunate ones. To this day, whenever I recall my early days in television, I still feel grateful that when I broadcast the Gillette Blue Blade commercials during three World Series, they were on radio only. Gillette's reluctance to put a razor in my hand on live TV may have saved a career — and a life.

Chapter 2

Ice Economics —
a Net Gain

In a share-the-wealth sports business arrangement, it usually comes down to this for club owners: Which is more important — winning or making money?

I first sensed the answer when I began televising New York Rangers hockey games in 1954. Sitting near me in the press box was Joe Schaefer. He was the team's official statistician and a passionate hockey fan who, at times, might serve as the penalty timekeeper, or the goal judge, or even final arbiter on who received credit for goals or assists.

But all of these responsibilities camouflaged Joe's most intriguing role, one that could directly affect the outcome of the game.

The mild-mannered member of the press box, with his well-sharpened pencils in evidence, was in reality a Superman of sorts, ready at a moment's notice to shed his civilian garb and, with a single bound, leap out of the press box and emerge on the ice as a National Hockey League goalie, an equal-opportunity net-minder ready to play for either team.

This was no fantasy. Joe Schaefer served as the house

goalie for the Rangers, or their opponent, should an injury occur putting either goalie out of action for the remainder of the game.

Did Schaefer have any professional experience? None at all, although when not working on statistics, he played as an amateur goalie with various clubs throughout the New York area.

But, you might ask, wasn't there a backup professional goalie, a second goalie on each team ready to take over if needed in the middle of a game? The answer is no.

NHL teams in the old six-team league would spring for only one goalie on the payroll. Only if an injured goalie would be out for the next game as well would a backup be called up from the minors.

As funny as this system may seem now, it was standard operating procedure in the NHL from the 1950-51 season to the 1965-66 season, when teams were required to dress two goaltenders for each game. And before the 1950s, there wasn't even a house goalie; if a goalie were injured, a teammate who played another position had to step in and guard the net.

Schaefer became the Rangers' house goalie in the early 1950s. His regular livelihood was manufacturing business forms and envelopes — that job supported him, his wife, and their three daughters — but hockey was his dream. He could visualize the intense excitement of getting word from the bench, putting down his stat sheets, racing to the dressing room, hastily donning his equipment, and, then, before a packed house, emerging on the ice at Madison Square Garden as an NHL goaltender. Movies could be made of dreams like this.

The years went by, and Schaefer kept grinding away at his statistical ledgers and staying in shape. By the time 1960 rolled around, Schaefer was 34 and too many Nedick's hot dogs had added pounds to his frame and a slight paunch to his figure. But on the night of February 17th, the alarm finally sounded and Schaefer answered the call.

It was 33 seconds into the second period. Chicago's Bobby Hull came swooping in on goal and got off a typical bullet shot that Gump Worsley sprawled to block. Hull's momentum carried him into Worsley, and one of Hull's skates cut two tendons in the goalie's stick hand. The blood was coagulating on the ice while Schaefer was racing down the steps from the press box to the dressing room. He was lacing up his skates as Worsley was being carted off to St. Clare's Hospital.

The Rangers were leading, 1-0, when Schaefer took over in the nets, the first native New Yorker to play for the Rangers or, for that matter, in the NHL. What a story it would have been if Schaefer had held the fort, but it was not to happen. He made some great saves, but not enough of them. New York couldn't score again while Chicago was pumping in five goals to skate off with a 5-1 victory.

Schaefer vowed that given another chance, he'd do better. A year later, on March 8th, the opportunity came.

Once again, it was Hull versus Worsley. This time, the Golden Jet came in on a breakaway. Worsley's leg shot out to block a blistering Hull wrister. The result? A hamstring tear, and Schaefer was back on the ice.

The Blackhawks were leading, 1-0, when Schaefer took over at 13 minutes and nine seconds of the first period. From there, to the final buzzer, he battled Chicago on even terms with an excellent effort. Each team scored three goals from that point on, and Schaefer finished with 27 saves. The Blackhawks won, 4-3, but it was a dream fulfillment for the veteran stat man. He had proved to himself, and others, that he could do the job.

That proved to be Schaefer's last appearance on NHL ice, although he continued as the house goalie until the rule change in 1965. And he remained as statistician until 1986.

Schaefer received $10 a game to handle both the statistics and serve as the standby goalie. That breaks down to $5 a game for each side with the stats thrown in for free. Schaefer received an additional $100 for each of the two NHL games he played in — more a floor covering than a salary cap. Obviously, finances were the owners' primary consideration, but like other house goalies who played during those years, Schaefer called his NHL on-ice experience "the thrill of a lifetime."

There were no thank-you letters or farewell ceremonies when Schaefer retired after 40 years at the Garden. But he and his wife, who now live in Ladson, South Carolina, have their scrapbook, their memories, and a unique place in NHL records. You can look it up.

And I'll never forget it. For it was one of my first lessons in management economics — the house goalie who, in the same game, first kept, and then became part of the official stats.

Chapter 3

LIFE at the Ballpark

Three years after I broadcast the perfect game — the Don Larsen no-hitter — I had an opportunity to broadcast another unique baseball scenario, a story with a smash ending. Hitting was the key to this drama though, not pitching, with all eyes focused on the Idaho strongman, Harmon Killebrew, on his way to becoming 1959's home-run leader in the American League.

Harmon swatted 42 round-trippers that season and experienced no difficulties in conquering cavernous Griffith Stadium in Washington, DC. That was a capital gain for the Senators, as Harmon's prodigious feats brought excited crowds to the ballpark.

I was behind the television mike for the play-by-play, watching the media coverage grow, homer by homer. One day, the announcement came that the nation's most widely-viewed publication, *LIFE* magazine, was joining the parade. Its staff was arriving for a picture-spread on the country's newest athletic sensation.

Understand that, in the 1950s, being pictured in *LIFE* was an athlete's greatest claim to fame. This slick pictorial weekly was the printed version of today's television news coverage.

LIFE camera crews were clicking away all over the country, zeroing in on the nation's biggest stories. Its only competitor was *LOOK* magazine, a distant second. *LIFE* maintained its exalted position at the top of the picture-weeklies until television's more timely coverage dealt a setback to the print version.

LIFE arrived in its usual grandiose style for the Killebrew extravaganza. No shoot-and-run coverage, theirs was a planned all-out offense with the only limiting consideration being the weekly deadline.

LIFE's first gambit was to lay down white tape from home plate to every spot in the bleachers where Killebrew's mammoth blasts had landed. From up above, it looked like the routes of coast-to-coast airlines. That may be what *LIFE* had in mind when it sent a cameraman up in a helicopter to take the aerial view.

Step two of the operation was to send a cameraman and reporter to Harmon's home for human interest stories and family pictures with his wife Elaine and their children.

Phase three was the hiring of crack picture-taker Dick D'Arcy of the *Washington Post* for an assignment necessitating great skill and perfect timing. Dick's battle station was right beside me in the open television booth behind home plate. His mission, from over 400 feet away, was to snap the shot at the precise moment that Killebrew's next blast landed in the bleachers or in a fan's eager hands, while capturing the anxious faces of surrounding bleacherites watching the ball's arrival. This took delicate timing and a perfect touch. One chance, no more, to press the shutter. Dick took up his vigil.

But that wasn't all. In left field, another photographer

would be focusing on the Killebrew swing, shooting 24 frames a second to record forevermore that magnificent, powerful follow-through.

The scene was set. I informed the TV audience that Harmon was scheduled to be featured in the upcoming issue of *LIFE* magazine, a keepsake for all his fans.

Everything was in place, the weather was perfect — all that was needed was a Killebrew home run. The text had been written, the photographers were on alert, the presses set to roll as soon as Harmon came through.

Problem was that the home-run express stalled. Dick D'Arcy waited, his camera poised, the cameraman shooting towards home plate remained ready; but after three days of homer famine, I no longer mentioned that *LIFE*'s story was still in the making. Would this be a long drought? Would Harmon come through?

Then, unbelievably, it all came together. A distinguished fan arrived unexpectedly at Griffith Stadium to watch an afternoon game. The President of the United States, Dwight Eisenhower, was among those watching Killebrew in action.

And Harmon delivered with deadline-time running out at the magazine. He crushed a towering drive deep into the left-field seats. Dick D'Arcy, with steady hands and keen eyes, snapped his picture at the precise moment that the ball landed while fans were scrambling for the souvenir. Dick gave me a vigorous thumbs-up salute signifying that he clicked away right on target. My call reflected the excitement and enthusiasm of the big moment, and my joy that Dick's timing was perfect. After the game I heard that the left-field photographer not only had an excellent shot of Harmon's swing, but to top it all off, had the perfect closer to the piece. He had swung his camera over to photograph the President standing and applauding just as Harmon trotted right by him on the way to the dugout.

That was worth waiting for. Harmon and the President. What a script! Everything clicked in every way.

"Look for the next issue of *LIFE*," I again reminded my viewers. "The picture story will be a collector's item."

And for those who treasure baseball classics, there's no doubt that the forthcoming issue of *LIFE* was extremely satisfying. But Killebrew was not in it. Instead, the magazine featured a record-setting pitching duel in Milwaukee where Harvey Haddix pitched 12 perfect innings before losing to Lew Burdette in the 13th, 1-0. This late-breaking story knocked Killebrew, his home runs, and all those great pictures right out of the box, and straight into *LIFE*'s files, never to rise again. The Killebrew story perished there, soon old and outdated and, as you know, *TIME-LIFE* marches on.

It took Harmon three turndowns, before this modest, humble player deservedly made the Hall of Fame. I've always believed the process might have been speeded up if the selectors had seen the never-published *LIFE* layout. Regardless, that presidential homer remains in my memory, a perfect baseball ending that I broadcast, but the nation never viewed.

There's a postscript to the Harvey Haddix masterpiece that canceled the Killebrew pictorial.

The story almost didn't get completed in time for publication because the final score wasn't decided until the day after the game when National League President Warren Giles decided it was 1-0, not 2-0 or 3-0 as originally believed.

Seems that in the 13th inning with two men on base due to an error, a sacrifice, and an intentional walk, Joe Adcock came up to the plate with the chance to win it for the Braves. Ironically, five years earlier it was Adcock who had lined a shot off Haddix's knee when the little lefty was pitching for the Cardinals. This blow not only damaged a nerve in Haddix's leg, it also shattered his chances for a 20-win season and changed his pitching style for the rest of his career. On this night, though, his 36-retired-in-a-row style was extraordinary.

And here was Joe Adcock up again. This time Adcock drilled a three-run homer to right field to win the game and end Haddix's fantastic pitching feat. Only it wasn't a three-run homer.

On the drive, Felix Mantilla scored, but Hank Aaron, believing that Adcock's liner had bounced over the wall for a ground-rule double, cut across the diamond without touching third base or the plate, and was passed by Adcock.

The next day Warren Giles ruled that Aaron was out for leaving the basepaths, and Adcock — his homer now a double — was out for passing Aaron on the bases.

Haddix later recalled he didn't know for a day whether the score was 3-0, or 2-0, or 1-0, nor did he realize that his 12 innings had been perfect without a walk. The *Pittsburgh Sun-Telegraph*'s headline proclaimed, "Haddix Hurls Greatest Game of All Time." It was an amazing performance.

And that's what it took to beat out Harmon Killebrew for the *LIFE* sports story of the week. A plaque commemorating the Haddix game resides in the Hall of Fame. Harmon eventually made it through election.

Chapter 4

"The Greatest Football Game Ever"

I couldn't believe my eyes. I was on the way to New York, going over my last-minute notes before my broadcast of the 1958 Giants-Colts National Football League championship game, and there it was in the *Baltimore News-Post*; the play-by-play story *written 24 hours before* the game.

TV personality Maury Povich, then my college-age assistant, watched me sit up with a start. "Maury," I said, "this is unbelievable. John Steadman has given himself the green light to write the game details even before the kickoff. This is spooky. John's writing who boots the ball, who returns it, who makes the tackle, and where the ball is spotted. The whole game in advance. How can anybody, especially a man of John's reputation, put his neck on the line like that?"

There was no question of the ability of Steadman, the paper's sports editor, to lure readership, though. The Colts were more than a football team in 1958. They were a religious crusade uniting every Baltimorean who, for years, had suffered the taunts of those who visualized their blue-collar fans as sweaty, beer-guzzling blowhards.

The Colts featured tough guys with crewcuts, missing teeth, and battered noses, the legacy of coal miners, truck drivers, and stevedores. Some had sampled the niceties of college life, but few had lingered in the classroom. College was something to be used only for player introductions.

"And from North College, at 290 pounds, No. 76, Big Daddy Lipscomb." Seems that Big Daddy, on his questionnaire, had listed "No College." Someone had added a period after No and the abbreviation provided Big Daddy with an alma mater.

The Colts were led by Johnny Unitas, who in 1956 had been a weekend semipro football quarterback. It took a phone call and a $6,000 salary to grab him. Raymond Berry was his most accomplished partner. But there were many more, all legendary Colts: Ameche, Donovan, Moore, Mutscheller, Marchetti, just to name a few.

The Giants, too, had players whose fame still shines bright. Names like Conerly and Gifford, Huff and Robustelli, Summerall and Webster. The list goes on.

The Giants had tradition; there was an aura of nobility about the team. Yankee Stadium, New York City, Broadway. Just the right setting for a championship game.

And, ironically, it was the Giants' sportsmanship that insured that the game was labeled the greatest ever played. There were no New York alibis in defeat, no disparaging remarks. Just praise and the constant refrain, "What a game to play in, win or lose."

❖ ❖ ❖

On December 28th, a crowd of 64,185 crammed into Yankee Stadium. And as with any good drama, the game built minute-by-minute to a stirring climax.

The Colts led at halftime, 14-3, but the game turned in the third quarter when the Colts picked up a first down on the Giants' three-yard line, but couldn't score. Then Conerly completed a long pass to Kyle Rote, who fumbled on the Colts' 25. Webster picked up the loose ball, was hauled down on the one, and Triplett burst in for the touchdown. The Giants trailed, 14-10, and the crowd roar increased.

Just after the fourth quarter began, Conerly connected with Gifford on a 15-yard touchdown pass and the venerable stadium exploded. The Giants led, 17-14.

With a little more than two minutes left, the Giants had the ball at their 43, fourth down and just inches to go. New York punted, and the Colts had their last chance, taking over on their 14 with one minute 56 seconds to play. In a relentless race against time, Unitas proved his greatness. His unerring passes dissected the Giants' defense; a final stirring catch by Berry, good for 22 yards, moved the ball to the New York 13. The seconds were ticking away. Steve Myrha raced onto the field. Nine, eight, seven, the kick was up and Baltimore fans erupted in shouting, cheering, and hugging. Myrha had sent the game into overtime.

The Giants received the overtime kickoff, but were forced to give up the ball. Unitas methodically piloted Baltimore to the title. In fact, he was so sure of his play selection that, on the six-yard line, instead of going for the winning field goal, he gambled on a sideline pass that moved the ball to the one. With one final burst of energy, the Colts' line opened up a gaping hole for Alan Ameche, who drove through with the game-winner.

I was limp at the end of the broadcast. The emotion was overwhelming. Two years earlier, I had broadcast the Don Larsen perfect game at Yankee Stadium, but that was individual achievement. The Colts were the champions and, of historical importance, the Colts had won the first overtime championship game in league history.

❖ ❖ ❖

The importance of the game went far beyond Baltimore and New York. The television and radio coverage had such a profound impact that the National Football League ascended that afternoon to a new pedestal. Networks, stations, fans, and advertisers clamored for more such heavy drama. Televised NFL football moved from being a game in America to a way of life.

In Baltimore, the outpouring of love and affection for the Colts was unprecedented in football history. Thirty thousand fans greeted them at the airport. The sponsor of my broadcast, the National Brewing Company, put out a highlight record that was played on newscasts every hour on the hour. The record was distributed as a promotion, and 10,000 copies were gone overnight. Every jukebox in town had my call blaring, "The Colts are the World Champions — Ameche scores!"

My statistician, Maury Povich, now hosts his own talk show, and Harry Hulmes, my spotter, is now the special assistant to the general manager of the Giants.

And as for John Steadman, who had the vision to write his game account before the outcome was known, the incredible happened. Almost everything in Steadman's story proved true in the most amazing feat of prognostication I've ever seen.

19

John's play-by-play vision included such highlights as the tieing field goal and the Ameche score. To top it off, he concluded his fictional account with the correct final score right on the button. Colts 23, Giants 17. The next day, the newspaper used its front page to congratulate him.

In Baltimore, the love affair with the '58 champions remained so torrid that when Steadman, in 1988, published his own book, titled *The Greatest Football Game Ever*, he sold out his first printing in three weeks.

"The marriage between the city and the Baltimore Colts is 30 years old," John wrote that year, "but remains the greatest love affair in sports."

Chapter 5

Big-Name Players

I always gave the score regularly when calling the Washington Senators' games. Of course, I didn't have to mention which team was winning or losing. Fans knew that in advance.

Sometimes, though, the Senators would win their opening game and experience the euphoria of leading the league. Reality was postponed for a day.

The fun was in fighting to get out of the cellar, or playing the role of spoiler in the pennant chase. There were always individual attainments to create excitement, and, regardless of crowd size, always plenty of noise. Half the spectators — transplanted Washingtonians — came out to whoop it up for their former hometown favorites. The Senators had their die-hard fans, many of whom I came to recognize by name. Stopping to chat as I walked up to the booth was like greeting family members. Just having big league baseball in any uniform was exciting. I rooted for each broadcast to be a good one, and let the base hits fall where they may.

Truth is, the Senators had some outstanding players — even some Hall-of-Famers and league leaders. Problem was, they just didn't have enough of them on any one team. Of course, those considered mediocre would have been million-aires on today's watered-down expansion clubs.

Dwelling on statistics of Washington players, except for a few stars, would have been a negative for TV viewers. More appealing were observations about the unusual personalities who gave the team its unique charm. Stories abounded on the telecasts, mixed in with the play-by-play, yielding to the baseball drama whenever the occasion demanded.

Little kids all knew the Shirley Povich line. The *Washington Post* columnist had expressed, "Washington — first in peace, first in war, and last in the American League." Nobody seemed nettled by this. The compensation was watching the artistry of the top big leaguers in action, most supplied by the invading teams. The Senators would score runs, but those other teams had the amazing ability to score even more. Strange how this happened so often. I learned never to say, "The Senators have a big lead going into the ninth." Why increase the frustration?

It wasn't that Washington lacked "big-name" players to talk about. Senators center fielder Carden Edison Gillen-water certainly was as big a name as any in the league — 23 letters in all. Now that's a big name. Granted that Mickey Mantle had more power, but you can't have everything. And there were others.

Let's start with the pitchers. Make room for Bobo Newsom. Bobo was the "neatest" pitcher in baseball. No, not "neatest" as in "coolest" or "outasight," but neatest in a literal sense. You see, Bobo was terribly fastidious in preserving an unblemished and tidy mound — the Felix Unger of his day.

Of course, all of this didn't go unnoticed. Opposing players would drive Bobo wild by scattering torn-up bits of scorecards, like so much confetti, all over his carefully-manicured plot on their way to the dugout. Bobo would not pitch until he bent over and picked up every speck of paper that sullied his domain.

Ever hear of a pitcher named Chuck Stobbs? One day in Washington, Stobbs uncorked a pitch that was not only past the batter, catcher, and umpire, but it also went sailing over the backstop, past the reserved seats, and finally landed up near some startled loungers in the mustard line at a hot dog stand. Might have been the longest wild pitch in the recorded history of baseball.

But Stobbs proved that he could set records in both directions. He also yielded a tape-measure, 565-foot home run to Mickey Mantle, a historic Griffith Stadium blast. Tell me, do you know any other pitcher who has gone so far in opposite directions? I later called another historic Mantle homer in Yankee Stadium — one that rocketed off the uppermost facing of the third deck in right field, halting its ascension to outer space. Off the Senators, of course. Pedro Ramos was the victim.

Then there was Hal Woodeshick. He was great when pitching to home plate. His only problem was in fielding a bunt or groundball and throwing to first.

Woodeshick was more than aware of his little problem. In fact, when forced to make a play to first, he would freeze in his tracks. Then, while standing there catatonically and being encouraged by his teammates to throw to first, Woodeshick would finally break out of his trance and, with an agonized cry, hurl the ball as though it were a live grenade.

And, of course, while the Washington right fielder chased after the ball and opposing players ran around the bases, we'd look forward to the relay and the play at third — sometimes even a play at the plate. It was exciting.

23

Washington fans were never bothered by Woodeshick's first-base phobia. After all, he could accurately throw to home, to second, and to third — and three out of four for a Senator was considered an excellent percentage.

My pitching staff also included Walt Masterson, one of the great pickoff artists in the game. (Washington opponents always seemed to have a man on first, so Walt had ample time to develop his specialty.)

Walt wore tinted spectacles on the mound, surveying potential basestealers through rose-colored glasses. Would-be perpetrators never knew when he was staring at them. Thus armed with this camouflage, plus a "jitterbug" pickoff step he claimed to have perfected in a Philadelphia dance contest, Walt made getting on base a foolhardy mission.

Senators fans used to say with pride that, with Walt's dance hall training, he always seemed to be a step ahead of every opponent.

My catchers were Lou Berberet and Clint Courtney. I first became enamored of Berberet the night he settled under a foul pop, threw his mitt off to one side, and calmly tried to catch the ball in his mask. Unfortunately, it wasn't allowed.

Clint Courtney was the first major league catcher to wear glasses. He was also the absolute best at getting thrown out of a game without saying a word. Clint would never question the umpire's call. He would simply register, while crouching behind the plate, his displeasure by drawing a line in the dirt with his finger. After each missed call, Clint would repeat the procedure, drawing a slash through the first four lines when the toll mounted to five.

That slash usually coincided with the ump's boiling point. All of a sudden, with an enraged bellow, the ump would holler,

"Courtney, you're gone!" and the innocent-acting catcher would turn around to inquire meekly what the problem seemed to be.

My first baseman? Norm Zauchin. Zauchin stumbled over a low railing while pursuing a foul ball one afternoon and landed in a lady's lap. The female fan promptly threw the ball back, but decided to keep Norm. In fact — so the story goes — they later married.

At second base, my choice was Tommy Upton, the resident bard of the Senators. One day in an interview before a spring training game, I coaxed Upton into reciting four lines of Shakespearean verse he had memorized for a college class. By the time the Senators arrived in Washington for Opening Day, the story had grown a bit. Upton was now being heralded as one of the great Shakespearean scholars of our time.

Alas, poor Upton, he couldn't hit as well as he could recite. He did field well, so fans sort of granted him poetic license when his batting average went from bat to verse.

The shortstop position went to Yo-Yo Davalillo. Actually, Yo-Yo — whose name accurately described his up-and-down career in the majors — made his presence known in Washington not with his bat or glove, but with his lips. Yo-Yo didn't speak English very well, but oh, how he could whistle. His piercing chirps echoed all over the usually half-empty ballpark. Talk about whistling while you work, Yo-Yo was the master.

Rocky Bridges held down third. Like Upton and Yo-Yo, Rocky would play a variety of positions. But wherever Rocky played, Rocky stood alone. Since he was the world's greatest tobacco chewer, nobody ever got close to him.

Rocky had the ability to load both cheeks at the same time — which made him a threat from both sides. He once confided that his double-barreled approach gave him better balance in the field and increased protection at the plate. Certainly, such a talent was nothing to spit at.

Flanking Carden E. Gillenwater in the outfield was left fielder Ernie Oravetz. Ernie was only 5'6" and wore thick glasses, but he stood tall. I can still visualize little Ernie competing against all those visiting musclemen power hitters, like a modern-day David against Goliath.

Right fielder — Albie Pearson. Even shorter than Oravetz, Albie collared a Rookie-of-the-Year Award for his play. But his baseball ability was only incidental. Albie was the lead singer in the "Singing Senators," a vocal group I organized that performed coast-to-coast on NBC-TV in the 1950s. In fact, Albie might have been the best vocalist baseball has ever produced; he certainly was always tops on my "hit parade."

Those are just a few of the delightful personalities who added zest to the broadcasts. These Senators all had talent — some even with a bat and a ball. I enjoyed them all during those happy years in Washington.

During that age of innocence, winning wasn't everything. Preferable, of course, but not vital to a fulfilling day at the ballgame. There was no discussion of salaries, no agents, drugs had not invaded the sports world, and there was no need to report how players were acting away from the ballpark. Those who drank too much were subjects for humor, not pity.

Players roomed together, spent time in hotel lobbies discussing their sport with fans, enjoyed giving autographs, spoke at youngsters' banquets without pay, understood that their dress and demeanor would serve as a guide to kids who idolized them, and realized how fortunate they were to have been blessed with professional talent. They played with a genuine love of the game, and a loyalty to the team they played for. Nice guys.

Today, professional players are part of the sports business. Big money has entered the picture along with its attendant evils. Now sports shows and sports sections keep tabs on drug cases, lawsuits, fines, suspensions, police blotter activity, rapes and assaults, renegotiating contracts, boorish behavior, refusal to play, goonery, trash talk and unsportsmanlike actions, along with the scores and standings.

This is all part of the reportorial scene, along with strikes, lockouts, and salary caps.

Sports used to be called fun and games.

The games continue.

Let the fun return.

Chapter 6

No Business Like Snow Business

The fear first gripped me when I entered the elevator in the Empire State Building. It was a solo ride to the 83rd floor.

I kept thinking, "If I don't pull this off, I'll make a fool of myself, but if I do make it work, I may never get to travel to a sports event ever again, and my broadcasting colleagues will have to stay at home, too."

In just half an hour, the Knicks' game from Cincinnati would be televised on WOR-TV, Channel 9 in New York. But there would be no announcer in Cincinnati to do the broadcast. I was sure of this, because I was the announcer. I had planned for everything in my helter-skelter schedule, except for that unexpected element — the weather.

March 5, 1966, was a cold, bleak day in New York. It would be a tense one as well. At noon my wife drove me to the Rose Hill Gym on the Fordham campus where, two hours later on NBC, I would be doing the play-by-play of the Eastern College Athletic Conference basketball Game-of-the-Week between the Rams and Manhattan College.

"I'll meet you right here after the game, Jane," I said. "Unless the game runs into overtime, I'll have over an hour to get to LaGuardia to catch the Cincinnati plane."

Somehow, I had always been able to fulfill all broadcasting obligations, no matter how close the time schedule, although past experiences had been tough on my nerves and my pocketbook. Like the day I broadcast a football game from Penn State in the afternoon, took a waiting taxi to a small airport near the stadium, flew in a rented aircraft to Boston, and sped to the Boston Garden just in time to announce the opening face-off in the Bruins-Rangers game.

On one blustery Saturday night in New York, I arrived at the snowbound airport after broadcasting the Knicks' game only to find that all flights had been canceled. I fulfilled my commitment on the Sunday Chicago Bears-Baltimore Colts assignment, however, by going to the train station and taking a midnight coach to Washington to get away from the snow. The rest was easy. From the train station I went to National Airport, where I shaved, changed clothes, ate breakfast, and flew to Chicago in time for the kickoff.

Somehow, things have always worked out, but as I looked out the window at halftime of the Fordham-Manhattan game, I had the sinking feeling that this time, for the first time, I might not be so lucky. Snow was coming down, and the sky was dark. The Knicks' broadcast was due to begin at 8 P.M. There was no color analyst standing by to help out. I was the lone announcer.

Fordham won the game, 82-72, and I was on my way to the airport in snow and fog. My wife had the radio on. Reports were already coming in of traffic snarls, blocked roads, and highway accidents. "Are the planes taking off? Are there delays?" I waited for answers to my questions, knowing they could have a vital bearing on my career.

"If the commercial planes are grounded or delayed, maybe I can hire a private plane to take me there," I told Jane. "Any long delays will kill me. My last chance will be American's flight 383, which will get me to Cincinnati with 35 minutes to go before airtime. It will take me about half an hour to get from the airport to Cincinnati Gardens, giving me five minutes to get to the mike. But if that one's delayed too, I've had it."

The airport was ominously quiet when I arrived. Many would-be passengers had either stayed home or left. The board was dotted with cancellations and held-up flights. A flight agent told me my chances would be better in the morning. I raced to a phone and called a charter service. Maybe I could find a pilot who would be willing to risk it. No answer.

Back to the counter. Waiting. And when quarter to six came and went, I knew it was over. I could no longer get there in time.

I turned to my wife. "Now's the time for inspiration. What shall I do?"

Jane smiled. "I know how you can do the game without even going to Cincinnati," she said.

"Yeah, how?"

"Just go over to Channel 9, sit in front of a TV set, and do it off the monitor."

As I got off the elevator at the 83rd floor, I had my plan all figured out. The viewers could watch the game, be able to check the scoreboard and the time, hear all the crowd roar and the public address announcer. I would supply comments from New York just as if I were at courtside.

Two final arrangements had to be made. First, I needed a

telephone by my side, next to the television set. Second, the other end of that phone had to be manned by someone at the game in Cincinnati. That someone was to be Frank Blauschild, then public relations director for the Knicks. I told Frank to fill me in on any notes or statistics that the camera did not cover.

My working area was a tiny cubicle termed an "announce booth." I sat there staring at a small television screen, ready for my call of the game. Richard Quodomine, the chief engineer, made sure I had a cutoff switch so that if I asked Frank a question such as "who's coming off the bench?" that query would not go over the air.

It was just before airtime. I considered my opening remarks. I did not want to make a public confession that I was not able to get to the game. As far as I knew, there were no rules stating that I had to explain my whereabouts. Yet journalistic honesty compelled me to make an acknowledgment that circumstances were different.

The red light was on. "Tonight's game is coming to you from Cincinnati with the audio being transmitted from the WOR-TV studios high up in the Empire State Building. Good evening, everybody, this is Bob Wolff with tonight's Knicks-Royals game. As you look at your television screen you'll see that pre-game ceremonies are about to begin honoring Jack Twyman. We'll pick these up from the P.A. system and then I'll be with you for the starting lineups and the call of the game."

I snapped the audio switch off. "Frank, are you there? Good, tell me the lineups please."

It was a terrific game. Overtime, no less. Cincinnati won, 149-145. Twyman, who was retiring at the age of 31, starred on this night with 39 points, his season high. It may have been the purest broadcast I have ever done. With no distractions, I was forced to comment only on what I saw on the screen.

"Good rebound position there by Bellamy, wasn't it?...What a beautiful pass by the Big O. He sure has a lot of assists tonight." (Switch off. 'Frank, how many assists for Robertson?')... "Just checked. Five more assists for Robertson and he ties his career high of 22." Incidentally, Oscar did just that along with scoring 44 points, including seven clutch ones in overtime.

It was a little lonely sitting there by myself for three hours, shouting into the mike from time-to-time. Many of the comments were the kind I would make in my living room, although I am not in the habit of speaking to myself. Game over, I again alluded to where the audio was coming from, picked up my folder and went home. No one ever knew the difference.

I kept my mouth shut about it, and, for sports broadcasters, that can be tough. I certainly did not want the day to come when future road trips might be a subway ride to a New York television studio. Nor did I want my colleagues to suffer a similar fate if travel costs became a factor.

So why did I come out of my Channel 9 closet 15 years later? I confessed my studio whereabouts in a *New York Times'* story only after NBC-TV proclaimed that the network was going to "experiment for the first time doing a football game without an announcer actually being at the game, using Bryant Gumbel for studio comments and updates." Now that this was going to be attempted on a national basis, I could no longer be accused of being the trendsetter.

Their experiment received great publicity, but play-by-play excitement was missing. Next time they might consider adding a studio play-by-play man with a phone connection to a perceptive assistant in the press box, along with a higher crowd noise level, and a louder public address announcer.

And, oh yes, I hate to admit this, but if weather conditions ever demand similar emergency tactics, the truth is it definitely can be done, and I'm not sure that anyone would notice the difference.

Chapter 7

Hit Man

You know all about the agony of defeat; now consider the agony of victory. I've spent years broadcasting sporting events, and no one I've seen fits that phrase better than Ron Hunt. Hunt, who retired in 1974, was, at that time, the major leagues' leader, career and season, for times hit by a pitch. He made his mark on baseball because 243 baseballs made their mark on him — 50 in one season alone. When it came to hard knocks, Hunt had no equal.

At an old-timers' game he explained the strategy behind his unusual method of getting on base.

Q: When did you develop this talent?

A: I started out with the Mets, then played for the Dodgers, but perfected my technique while I was with the San Francisco Giants. Nobody wanted to put me on base — not with Willie Mays, Willie McCovey, Jim Ray Hart, and Jim Davenport right after me.

Q: How did you work at it?

A: I spent a lot of time in front of the mirror. I used to check myself out as far as turning away from the ball, making it look as if I were getting out of the way while still covering the plate very well with my arms and my rear end. Also it helped to blouse my uniform a little bit more and wear baggier pants.

Q: Where did you take most of those hits?

A: In the ribs, in the back. Anytime they threw a slow curveball, I'd try to get a tick on the arm.

Q: How did this affect your hitting?

A: I was having a little trouble with the inside pitch. By crowding the plate, I'd take the tight one away from the pitcher. I could now use the inside pitch to get hit, and cover the rest of the plate with the bat. But I was never called back by an umpire for getting hit intentionally.

Q: How many inches did you blouse out your uniform?

A: Well, instead of wearing a normal size 36 shirt, I'd put on a 44 or 48 and blouse it four or five inches. I had a long tail on my shirt so it wouldn't come out.

Q: How about the pants?

A: I just got balloon-type pants. It was fine until the double knits came in.

Q: There wasn't much time, with the pitch on the way, to think "hit or be hit," was there?

A: My thinking took place before the ball was thrown, offensively and defensively. Once the ball was on the way, I programmed myself to react. If the pitch was in the area of my shoulder or my rear end or my leg area, I got hit. If it was over the plate, I tried to hit it.

Q: What about the pain?

A: It hurt, of course, but I found I could absorb more pain than the other guy. I perfected my ability to give a little with my body when the ball hit, to take away some of the shock.

Q: Didn't you have a lot of injuries?

A: No. Denny Lemaster hit me in the hamstring, and

while I was trying to maintain my balance, I pulled it. That cost me three or four weeks. When I was with the Giants, Tom Seaver hit me in the head. The ball went so high in the air they could have called it an infield fly. At the hospital, the X-rays showed nothing. Except for a few broken bones in my hands, that was it. Nothing serious.

Q: Didn't any of the top fastball pitchers scare you just a bit?

A: No. Gibson, Koufax, Drysdale — all those guys threw hard. I wasn't concerned.

Q: Whose pitch hurt the most?

A: I guess it was Drysdale's. His ball would tail in and just keep coming at you. The rest of them — well, they all threw hard, but that was not going to influence my decision as to whether I'd get in the way of the ball or not.

Q: From a counterstrategy standpoint, did pitchers avoid coming inside to you?

A: Yeah — I scared some of them who couldn't pitch inside with confidence. Seaver, I know, threw at me a couple of times on purpose. In fact, I ran into him at an old-timers' game up in New York, and he wanted to take batting practice before the game. I said to him, "I'll throw to you." Seaver said, "Nothing doing. You'll hit me." I told him, "You bet I will."

Q: How long did it take after you were plunked to throw off the pain?

A: I never even thought about it.

Q: Where did you prefer to be hit?

A: From the shoulder blades to above the waist, the kidney area. The buttocks also were a good place. The legs, the elbows, the head — those were the worst places.

Q: If your remarkable career were to get you into the Hall

of Fame, what memento would you like to have on display at Cooperstown?

A: My bat handle — good as new. No inside pitch ever hit it.

Q: Looking back on your career, who stands out most in your mind?

A: Casey Stengel. A great man. He told us if we were ever troubled by something to come to him. I was a second baseman by trade, but when I first came to the Mets I spent seven games as a bullpen catcher. I went to Casey and said, "I want to play." "You really want to play that bad?" said Casey. "Yes, I do," I said. Casey said, "O.K. You'll play tomorrow." That's how I got my start.

Q: Anybody else?

A: Well, the president of the National League made a great impression on me — after all, his autograph was on the baseballs.

Chapter 8

Clubhouse Transactions

The center of attention at Yankee spring training camp in 1992 was pitcher Pascual Perez. The lanky righty from the Dominican Republic arrived in a limousine, emerged bedecked with jewelry, and, once in uniform, cavorted around the field, bestowing his smile, his cackle, and his frenetic presence on first one cluster of players, then another. Pascual played the house, and personified the exuberant adult playing a kids' game. The players flocked around him, responding to the Pied Piper.

I told my cameraman, "Just follow Pascual wherever he goes. He's the show. And make sure our mike picks up all the talk —and the laughter. His teammates love him."

When practice began, we trained our camera on Perez warming up on the sidelines. With long arms and legs geared into a distinctive pumping pitching style, he was the essence of grace and confidence. After Perez's workout concluded, I concentrated on others taking batting and fielding practice, but cut that short to seek out Perez for an interview before he left the clubhouse.

Perez was the Yankee story — energetic, enthusiastic — all I needed was a short interview to go along with my candid camera shots and my nightly TV feature would be completed, and hopefully memorable.

I finally found the righthander in the locker room, fully dressed in a colorful blue and red polo shirt, tan pants, sparkling jewelry around his neck and rings on his fingers. I surmised that, having worked out, he was being allowed to leave early, and I didn't want to miss my chance to put him on camera with me.

"Pascual, I just need a couple of minutes with you," I began. "I've already got you talking with your teammates; now all I need are a few comments from you. O.K.? Can I do it now just outside this room? That's where my camera is set up."

Perez, speaking broken English but seeming amenable to my request, gave me a rather standard spring-training put-off answer, "right afta I peech."

"But Pascual, you've already pitched," I countered. "We have that on tape. Just give me a minute — that's all I need."

"Afta I peech, I do show. I do it."

"Pascual, we have to leave to get this tape back. Do you plan to pitch this afternoon? We can't stick around for that."

"No, I peech now. Take a minute."

"You're going to pitch here?"

"No, there," he said, pointing to the trainer's room. And then seeing my perplexed look, he suddenly grabbed his crotch and shouted, "I gotta peech — I gotta peech, you understand?"

"Oh, you gotta piss. Of course, go to it. We'll wait."

I got the interview, but that "peech" was Perez's last as a Yankee. It proved to be one requested by the commissioner's office. Pascual flunked his drug test, and it ended his career in New York. He was soon gone both from the camp and, until 1996, from organized baseball; but the memory lingers on.

❖ ❖ ❖

Al Lopez was one of my favorite managers. A man with class, charm, and a friendly, relaxed manner, he would spend the same time with me when I was a rookie broadcaster as he would with the celebrated journalists. That was appreciated. I tried to follow a similar policy, making sure to interview rookies as well as stars.

In the late 1950s when I had my filmed syndicated program show playing in selected major league cities, I kept an anxious eye on the transaction news making sure that none of my interviews would feature a player who had just been traded or let go. That would have been the height of embarrassment.

Chicago knuckleballer, Paul LaPalme, a crafty lefty, was my scheduled guest on a Yankee pre-game show on WPIX, New York. On Thursday I heard the rumor that he might be released. LaPalme's show was slated for Saturday afternoon. I had to find out quickly whether he'd still be with the White Sox when the show aired.

The Chicago skipper took my phone call, and I explained the situation. "Al, I really have a problem with this one. I don't know what you plan to do with LaPalme, but he was a solid performer when I filmed him earlier this year, and I figured I'd be safe. Unfortunately, I have no replacement program in New York. I'm really sweating this out. Will he still be with you on Saturday?"

There was a long pause, then the "Senor" as we called him, asked a telltale question. "Bob, what time does your show go on?"

"1:15, Al, just before the ballgame."

"1:15, Bob? That means it's over at 1:30 on Saturday, is that right?"

"That's right, Al."

Another pause.

"O.K., Bob, breathe easier. I'll take care of you."

"My thanks, Al. I'll never forget it."

The press announcement about La Palme's release came out that day at 3 P.M.

❖ ❖ ❖

"Bob, come down to the end of the bench with me — I want to ask you a question."

I followed the Senator's bespectacled catcher, Clint Courtney, to a spot near the bat rack, and inquired, "What is it, Clint?"

"I'm having a little trouble with my throwing. I thought you might come out to the park with me early tomorrow and help me practice."

"Sure, Clint, I'll help you, but what's the problem?"

"Well, it's throwing back to the pitcher. I don't know what's wrong. Sometimes I'm high, sometimes low, or off to one side or the other — it just doesn't come naturally for some reason. I don't want to make a poor throw in a game, and thought maybe I could practice with you. I just have to get the feel back."

"Sure, Clint. I'll help you work that out. Just don't worry about it. I'll be there all set to go."

I worked out daily with the Senators, and filled in, when available, pitching batting practice. That's where Clint wanted to use me — as a pitcher.

"Just let me keep throwing back to you," Clint said, "so it's second nature again, and I can put the ball where I want it."

I became the willing target, advised Clint to just snap the throws back to me chest-high, right at the letters, until it became a repeated rhythm. And for a week, I threw, Clint caught, and back came the ball on a perfect line, chest-high every time.

"Clint," I said, "in my opinion you're cured. You're back in the groove. I wouldn't ever worry about your throwing again. It couldn't be better."

Clint muttered his thanks, but his pensive look told me he still had a concern.

"What is it, Clint?" I asked.

"Bob, I've practiced with you for a week, throwing everything back to your chest. What happens if I get a real tall or short pitcher with a different chest level — a different height — will this still work?"

"Clint, let me reassure you. A chest is a chest, doesn't matter to whom it belongs. You're cured for all bodies, big or small. Just believe me. You'll see for yourself. You're ready."

And so he was. The problem never returned.

Chapter 9

Word Games

I've never believed in being tabbed "the voice" of a team. I always felt this was slighting the second or third announcers who certainly lent their voices and talents to the game, too.

There were benefits to the billing, however, besides financial, and, among them, during the days of sponsor domination, was increased job security. When a new competing beer bought the broadcast rights, the ballclub could assure my employers that I had not been "the voice" of the previous brew. I was "the voice of the team," the vital factor in job longevity. This was mandatory word use to avoid going down the drain along with the suds of the former sponsor.

It helped considerably through a steady parade of Washington-sold beers, many of which worked to also gain footholds in towns outside the nation's capital. This included Gunther's, Old Georgetown, Senate, Valley Forge, National Boh, and many more.

Each beer had its own advertising agency, and its own marketing plan. Their job was to sell the beer — my job was to put forth an effective play-by-play broadcast and overall presentation. Combining both selling and broadcasting sometimes caused conflicts.

It's Not Who Won or Lost the Game—
It's How You Sold the Beer

When Gunther's came on the scene, with its marketing game plan, I had added some radio innings to my TV calls, and the advertising agency VP thought I was exactly the one to implement a new campaign. "With the stations on the network, we can gain a lot of goodwill in each city if we work in some mention of each town's landmarks — you know — libraries, banks, distinguished citizens, history — that sort of stuff. Good public relations will help our salesmen. We'll write the stuff for you. All you have to do is read it."

What he didn't tell me was these cards were going to be given to me to read at the most crucial parts of the game — "bases loaded, game tied, cleanup batter at the plate." In those key tense situations, listeners wanted baseball, not blurbs.

It was most difficult to work in historical material during play-by-play without intruding on the drama of the game. Can you imagine a similar digression at the key point in a movie, a stage show, or TV drama? I tried to explain to the account executive the listener resentment that would occur. With the excitement mounting, I'd be shifting to a travelogue. Fans would be indignant at this intrusion during key moments.

"You don't understand," the agency pundit assigned to feed me the promos, tried to explain, "They'll still get all the baseball information. We're just adding a little hometown tribute."

"You see," he continued, "I try to pick the most important spots in the game so we can reach the peak attentive audience. It's just good advertising technique, and you're part of the process. The decision has been made."

The listeners were irate, their phone calls poured in, and their mail escalated. Reasoning didn't seem to matter. The sponsor had complete control. Protests were brushed aside. A difficult situation was getting worse.

And then the showdown occurred. Sales in our home city, Washington, DC, were to receive a boost. A new promo had been written for our nation's capital.

Sure enough, at the crucial point in a home game, the agency representative handed me a card. "Now, read this," he whispered. I looked at the card, looked again, turned aside from the mike, and said to the ad man, "Please, I can't read that on the air. I'll explain later."

Booth war had been declared.

"Read it now — now."

"Let's discuss it first," I said off mike, holding the card.

The agency man stormed out of the booth, I finished the broadcast, and, later at my office, was handed a telephone message. I was to report to an emergency morning meeting at agency headquarters.

I didn't expect solitary confinement, but I knew my job could be on the line.

Surrounded by agency brass, I heard again an account of my insubordination, my refusal to play by their rules, my disdain of their selling methods, even hints of disloyalty to their prized brew.

Finally, having vented their wrath, they asked, "So what do you have to say?"

"Gentlemen," I said, "You can all thank me for having the presence of mind to rescue you from an embarrassing situation — one that would have reflected poorly on your ad copy and my common sense. I could not read that copy, and I said so to your representative. I told him I'd explain later, but he was gone."

"What's wrong with the copy?" thundered one of the more vociferous antagonists.

"Here's the card I was handed." I took it from my papers

and paused. "It says: 'Today I want to tell you about the biggest erection in Washington.'" I paused again, and then the room exploded with laughter.

I continued: "Our listeners would have had the same reaction. We all would have been laughed at. Fortunately, I was able to save us from that. I'm sure there are better ways and better times to identify the Washington Monument."

The meeting broke up shortly thereafter. Fortunately, it wasn't long before the irritating campaign came to an end.

I continue to believe that the national pastime should mean baseball.

Chapter 10

"Just Relax"

The race against time began when my home phone rang in mid-afternoon with a desperate caller on the line.

"Bob, I need a favor. You've got to help me," pleaded Mike DiTomasso, a former top-notch basketball official, whose whistle helped to pay his way through law school. Mike was then the producer and analyst on New Jersey Nets TV basketball games.

"What's the problem, Mike?"

"Bob, you know John Sterling. He's here with me to call the play-by-play tonight, but, Bob, he can't speak. He's got laryngitis. I know this is short notice, but it's an emergency. Can you possibly help us out?"

I checked my watch. It was 3:30. There'd be no time for proper preparation, but I could still cram in the basic essentials. I'd need player numbers, game notes, program format, a quick rundown on the starters and bench guys, up-to-date stats and standings, commercial cue lines, but, above all, time to get to the arena. If I started immediately before the heavy traffic, I'd have time to watch the warmups, and maybe get in a word with the coaches.

"I'll do it, Mike," I said. "Let's see — the Nets are playing the Bulls. That's fine. Should be fun. Just check them out for me on injuries, any guys I haven't seen, you know what I need. Please have all the numbers, notes, and the rest ready for me when I arrive. I'll shave quickly, change shirts, and should be at the Meadowlands around 5:30."

"Bob, hold on. I'm calling from Chicago. The game's in Chicago."

"Mike, you're in Chicago, and the game's tonight? I live outside New York and my home is about an hour from LaGuardia Airport. You're sure you want to chance this?"

"I need you. Start now. I'll be there at courtside."

And the race began.

I threw some stuff in an overnight bag. Jane went to get the car. Her driving would save me parking time. No time to call for a reservation. We were on the way. I arrived at the airport, jumped out of the car, raced into the terminal building, noted I had five minutes to make a flight, got a ticket, checked my overnight bag, ran to the gate, boarded the plane, and took the last empty seat.

So far, so good. What I was counting on was the one hour time difference. New York was an hour later. Maybe I could pull this off.

The plane rolled out on the runway — and then just sat there. Sat there. Immobile. I kept looking at my wristwatch. The minutes were ticking away, and I began to perspire. Finally, I pressed the button for the stewardess. "What's happening," I said, "when will we take off?"

"I'll speak to the captain," she said. I waited some more.

Finally, I heard a microphone click on. It was the pilot speaking. "At this hour there's always a lot of airline traffic," his communique began. "We're about 15th in line. So just sit back and relax."

"Just sit back and relax." Words that should be banned from the airlines. Nobody gets on a plane to sit back and relax. They get on to get someplace in a hurry. I was now a captive passenger, though, and a captive audience.

Problem is I couldn't relax even after we finally took off. I was up and running when we pulled into Chicago, bolted off the plane and left my overnight bag circling around on the conveyer. There was no time to pick up a Chicago newspaper to check out a pre-game story. What I needed above all else, was a taxi. I sped through the door to the taxi stand.

My heart sank. Over 50 people were already in a line waiting for the next available cab. This was a crusher.

Frantically, I raced into the middle of the incoming and outgoing airport traffic, waving my arms like a madman, searching for a police car.

And I finally spotted one. Or maybe he spotted me, jumping from side to side as cars went whizzing by.

"What's wrong, pal? What're you doing? What's all the fuss about?"

"Officer, am I glad to see you. I'm desperate." I explained my situation. "I have exactly 20 minutes to get to the Chicago Stadium to do the play-by-play on the Bulls-Nets TV game — and they're counting on me. My plane was late — I couldn't wait in line for a cab — and please I need your help."

"Jump in," said the officer, "here we go." He sounded his siren, put on his blinding front light, pulled up behind the first empty cab he saw, and motioned him over to the curb.

The startled driver rolled down his window. "Did I do something wrong?"

"Nothing to worry about, but this is important. Get this

man to the Chicago Stadium as quickly as possible without breaking the speed laws."

The driver nodded assent. I told the police officer I would be forever grateful, jumped into the cab, and away we went.

There was exactly one minute to go before airtime when the cab arrived at the arena.

I had his fare money waiting in my hand including a well-earned tip, hustled through the players' entrance, sped across the court, grabbed a player roster from Mike DiTomasso, and asked what my first cue would be.

There were 10 seconds left. I picked up the mike, took a breath, moved in front of the camera, and the red light came on. I was on the air.

"Hi everybody, I'm Bob Wolff and it's a pleasure to be with you here in Chicago as we bring you the New Jersey Nets against the Chicago Bulls."

I didn't add, "so just sit back and relax."

Chapter 11

Man in the Stands

It is Memorial Day, 1957, at old Griffith Stadium in Washington. The Yankees are playing a holiday doubleheader against the Senators. Between games, I left my booth and went downstairs in search of a guest for my radio interview.

Move back in time with me, switch on the radio and tune in.

"Hi, everybody, this is Bob Wolff with your pre-game interview brought to you by Todds and Amana air conditioners. Amana — the first big name in home air conditioning to let you match your air conditioner with the decor of your home. See Todds about the space-saving, central-cooling Amana air conditioner.

"On this pregame show I thought we'd do something new for a change. As you know, we've heard so much from the ballplayers, and the coaches and officials and the managers, I thought today just at random I'd go down and let you hear from some of the folks who are gathered here at Griffith Stadium to watch this big Memorial Day doubleheader. So I just sauntered down here, down in the first deck, and I think that I'll ask this first gentlemen here who has been watching how he's enjoying the game. 'Sir, how did you like the first game today?"

"Well, of course, being a Washington fan, I thought it was great. And, I particularly, of course, like everybody else, got a big thrill out of that homer Jim Lemon hit against the wind into those left-field seats."

"Well, these boys have been playing inspired ball. Have you had a chance to see many other games this season?"

"Well, I came out opening night — opening day — I saw the President throw the ball out that day, and Washington, as you recall, lost to the Yankees I believe — it was a pretty good game though. Otherwise, I've been seeing it on television. I've seen you, as a matter of fact, too, but as you know we haven't done too well. But I did see the game the other day on TV which started this winning streak — that is, the second game of the Baltimore doubleheader the other day."

"I see you brought your daughter with you today."

"Yes, and she has never seen a baseball game until today except on television, so this was a lucky day for her to see the winning game."

"Well, that's terrific."

"She also got a baseball signed by Cookie Lavagetto, so she's pretty happy."

"Isn't that wonderful! I see you are sitting pretty near the playing field. What'd you think of the pitching in the first game?"

"Well, of course, for Washington it was just great and we all know Washington's been having some tough luck with its pitching. I was particularly glad to see Pascual finally beat the Yankees, as I understand he's never beaten them before. And, of course, that relief pitching was tops, too, and against the Yankees this was something."

"Are you originally from Washington, sir?"

"No, I'm a Californian. I was and still am."

"Well, some of our boys on the team come from California."

"I just heard that several of them did. Lou Berberet I understand is. Rocky Bridges came from California. And then Bob Usher's been playing in San Diego I think. And they all did pretty well today, too."

"Well, that's great that you can be here all the way from California. Have you done much traveling around the country?"

"Yes, I've been in most of the 48 states at one time or another. And also I've traveled a bit abroad in the last few years."

"So you've had a chance to see quite a bit of baseball?"

"Well, not as much as I would like. I catch it whenever I can, but usually I must say I see it on television."

"Did you have a chance to do any playing of sports yourself?"

"Well, I'll tell you. I s'pose one of the reasons I like both baseball and football is that I went out and never made the team. So I like to watch others who can do it."

"I see. Well, how long have you been here in the nation's capital? For some time?"

"Well, off and on, I've been here about 10 years."

"Oh, well, you're practically a native right here now."

"Practically a Washingtonian by this time."

"I see. What sort of work do you do, sir?"

"I work for the government."

"For the government?"

"Yes, yes for the government."

"Oh?"

"My boss is President Eisenhower."

"Your boss is President Eisenhower? What sort of work do you do, sir?"

"Well, I'm the Vice President."

"Ladies and gentlemen, our guest has been the Vice President of the United States, Vice President Richard Nixon...."

I thanked him for being my guest, and then added, "We always give our guests Countess Mara neckties. I hope you enjoy this one."

"This is fine. I'm always in need of ties because I usually have to wear one."

Politics notwithstanding, good straight men are hard to find.

Chapter 12

Mom and Pop Operations

Nowadays in the sports field, you can't tell the vice presidents without a scorecard. But when I started out as a professional sportscaster, big league teams and organizations were run by a handful of people, sort of Mom and Pop organizations, like the corner stationery store. Today, owners prefer a first-name relationship to become one of the boys, but, in the early days, many sports tycoons enjoyed the courtesy of being called "Mister."

Clark Griffith, the feisty owner of the old Washington Senators, was one of my favorites. He had three passions — baseball, cards, and the Wild West, and he apportioned his day to include all three.

Mr. Griffith's morning was spent conducting baseball matters. Noon to 1 P.M. was an eat-in lunch with his large adopted family (they called him "uncle"), spinning baseball stories around a long, well-stocked table. From 1 P.M. to 4 P.M., back in the main room again, a mandatory pinochle card game was underway. Every merchant who wanted to do baseball business with "the Old Fox," from insurance salesmen to sign painters, to program printers, to concessionaires, to equipment suppliers of bats, balls, and gloves, realized he'd better sit in on this daily obligatory event if he wanted to preserve his present contracts or get future ones. It was always a full house.

At 4 P.M. the card game came to a halt, the room was cleared, and Mr. Griffith isolated himself in front of a radio, and in later years a television set, where he relived his childhood memories by listening to or watching "The Lone Ranger." Emerging refreshed after the bad man was captured, "Griff" had dinner, and then watched his beloved team struggle against odds, just like the Western pioneers of his early days.

As the team's telecaster and broadcaster, I was called upon to emcee social occasions, including Mr. Griffith's birthday parties at the stadium. I'll never forget the emotion at one of those cake-cuttings when I presented a personally recorded birthday salute obtained from the Lone Ranger himself, Clayton Moore. If I had produced a 20-game winner for the Senators, it couldn't have had more impact.

Mr. Griffith's baseball staff consisted of a few family members and a couple of long-time friends. The only scout I was conscious of was Joe Cambria, who divided his time between running a laundry in Baltimore and scouring Cuba for players. Communication was a problem. Manager Chuck Dressen often had to use a Cuban bullpen pitcher as interpreter. Chuck coached at third, and that proved to be difficult on those infrequent occasions when a Cuban Senator reached that base.

One night Carlos Paula thwarted a last-inning rally by trying to come home on an easy infield bounder. Paula haltingly explained in the locker room that Dressen had yelled "go." "I was misinterpreted," bellowed Dressen. "I yelled 'whoa.'"

Owners in the early days played prominent roles in their organizations. In his imperial manner, George Preston Marshall was at the helm of the Washington Redskins. GPM was called "Mr. Marshall" by his friends and foes alike, including his office staff, his uniformed chauffeur, his coaches, the media, and the telephone company that installed a direct line from his seat in Griffith Stadium to his team's sideline bench.

"Ever get any wrong numbers?" I asked in jest one day after bumping into the grim owner as I emerged from my play-by-play call in the Redskins' TV booth. Fixing me with an icy stare, he snapped, "Just wrong plays," ending my indelicate attempt at light conversation.

When I first joined Madison Square Garden, my broadcasting home for 36 years, it was operated by just a few executives and a small office staff. I began commuting from Washington to televise its sports events in 1954. General John Reid Kilpatrick, portly, stiff-collared, and impeccably groomed, was president of the Rangers in their six-team league.

Some of his scouting was done by radio, tuned to out-of-town games. The story goes, and I never dared to ask him to confirm it, that one night the general was tuned to a Montreal game and heard the French announcer talk about "LaRondelle," in action all over the ice. The general, impressed, sent an aide to Montreal to take a closer look at this marvel. The aide returned, mission accomplished, with the puck (la rondelle in French) in his hand.

Today's Garden, sitting above Pennsylvania station, is a sprawling complex in two separate buildings with 38 vice presidents at my last count, and hundreds of others hoping to attain the same status. As with other sports organizations, television money and the growth of cable have caused the big explosion from modest profits in gate receipts and hot dogs to the billion-dollar industry of sports entertainment and marketing by-products that exists today.

With modern times, many ideas remain the same, but the packaging has changed. For years, newspapers, TV, and radio resisted publicizing corporate sponsors. That was solved rather easily. The sponsors just bought the events and slapped on their corporate names as part of the deal. In recent years they've even bought the buildings. For additional exposure they arranged their signs so that the TV cameras were sure to focus on them. Sports heroes, and villains, too, became the most heralded television stars, along with their T-shirts, caps, sneakers, shirts, jackets, autographs, videos, and any other items that combine exposure with profits.

The burgeoning contracts brought out agents in hot pursuit of even larger salaries for their clients, intensifying the management-labor chasm, with the resultant spillover of dissatisfied players no longer willing to do or die for their teams unless being assured of landing in a soft cushion of greenbacks.

Sports psychologists entered the picture to try and keep these athletes on an even emotional keel. This idea may have been borrowed from the legendary baseball showman, Bill Veeck, who years ago hired Dr. David Tracy as a hypnotist with the old St. Louis Browns. Before Dr. Tracy appeared as my guest on a Washington post-game show, I suggested, as a humorous aside, he hypnotize my viewers into buying the brand of television sets sponsoring the program. The doctor was most willing to try this experiment, and, with the camera focused on him, he dangled a pendant back and forth as he soothingly advised our viewers that in the morning they should begin their day by going to their nearest appliance dealer and buying the new RCA television sets we were selling. It was a masterful performance.

The next morning the Federal Communications Commission called me and suggested that there be no more such salesmanship on TV, adding it received many calls from viewers who had been put to sleep watching my show. I assured the FCC it wasn't the good doctor, it was just that my late-night sports program was designed to relax viewers before they put out the lights, and sometimes they might even fall asleep during the show itself.

The increased sales I attributed to my increased viewership and the quality of the product. But I did agree with the FCC that it would be wise to have a rule preventing future use of hypnosis on television, and it could rely on my complete cooperation in that regard.

As for Dr. Tracy's results with the Browns, they were not able to pick up any extra wins. After all, talent is talent, but, frankly, they did seem happier losing.

With the expanded organizations of today, a sportscaster answers to many bosses, including network or station. In the early days it was the sponsor, but when pro football was becoming a major TV sport, the overseer was the top man himself.

Bert Bell, the raspy-voiced NFL commissioner, woke me at three o'clock one morning with his critique prior to the regular season. "Watched your TV game tonight," he growled, "and twice you called it 'an exhibition game.' We don't play 'exhibition games,' " he scolded, "we play 'pre-season games.' And don't use 'tripped' or 'wrestled' when a ball carrier goes down. Those are wrestling words and we're not plugging wrestling, we're selling football. Otherwise, good call."

Sportscasting remains the same subjective field, though, a mixture of journalism, name appeal, and show business in hiring practices. Some years ago I found that Frank Waldecker, an able commercial announcer on the Westminster Kennel Club Dog Show, had not been renewed. When I asked why, I was told "he wasn't the dog show type." I continued telecasting that event for 33 years figuring I must be "the type," and I still don't know whether that's a compliment or a doggone shame.

Chapter 13

The Assignment

Would you like to be a World Series broadcaster?

When I started my career, that was the number-one ambition shared by sportscasters. During the years, while broadcasting championships in all the major sports, I witnessed other finals rising to top-level status as well, but for many decades the World Series has been something special.

Of course, ambition to broadcast the Series is one thing, attainment another.

For years, four announcers, two on TV and two on radio, were chosen as follows: one would be selected from each competing team, a third would be a network choice, and the fourth would be named by the sponsor, Gillette. The sponsor had the final say on all four and would control the broadcast. The announcers would split the play-by-play on each medium, changing from first to last half on each game. There were no "analysts" or "color men." The professional announcer handled that as well.

In more recent years, the network alone has regained complete power and has made the announcer choices. Wresting control was made easier when increased rights fees opened up the door for a multitude of sponsors to share in the broadcasts. Now there's one play-by-play man, and one or two analysts on the network TV side, and, on network radio, one or two play-by-play callers and an analyst. The networks make the decisions. Competing teams and individual sponsors have no say.

For the first nine seasons while I did the play-by-play of the Washington Senators, I realized my chances were slim of realizing my World Series ambition. Chances were remote that Washington would be a league champion in my lifetime. That eliminated the contending-team announcer possibility. I was beginning to make TV and radio inroads on the networks, but still needed more backing there. That left one opening — making a favorable impression on Gillette.

The Gillette folks were friendly people, tremendous sports fans, and when the Senators played in Boston, I'd stop by from time to time to call on them at their home base and talk baseball. These were informal sessions, but somehow I always had the feeling I was auditioning.

I didn't believe it was politic to mention my desire to be with them on the fall classic. In fact, it would have been rather presumptuous and downright pushy. Didn't have to anyway; they certainly had to be aware of my feelings. Our conversations centered on stories about the day's sports news, and interesting personalities in the game.

One day at lunch, though, with Craig Smith, the Gillette advertising director and Al Leonard, their PR chief, they suddenly hit me with the big question.

"Bob, what's your ambition in baseball broadcasting?"

I hesitated, then came right out with it. "Well, that's easy to answer. I'd love to broadcast the World Series some day — that's always been my sportscasting dream — and I know I can do it — so I hope that I'll merit the chance. How does one qualify to join your team?"

"Well, Bob you're close, so don't despair. All you need is just a little bigger name."

"Gosh, that's a cinch. If I ever get on, I'll have a bigger name in 24 hours."

We laughed and the conversation turned elsewhere.

And then good luck played a vital role.

The All-Star Game was scheduled for July 10, 1956, in Washington's Griffith Stadium, my home park. Gillette decided they needed a Washington host announcer on the broadcast team for added local color. I was selected to share the play-by-play role — a major breakthrough. My chance had come.

In Washington, the crowd roar was usually equally divided between the home team and the opposition. Government workers from all over the country had a chance to root for their native cities, and the old stadium never lacked for noise. There was plenty to shout about in that '56 encounter. Three terrific fielding plays by third baseman Ken Boyer of the Cardinals, along with three hits, paced the National League to a 7-3 victory. In fact, the senior circuit scored five times before the American League got on the scoreboard in the sixth inning with back-to-back homers by Ted Williams and Mickey Mantle.

When I left the broadcast booth I knew I had given it my best effort and now could just hope it was well received. That verdict came in quickly. The Gillette folks were lavish in their praise, and the phone calls, letters, and print reviews were most laudatory. It was exhilarating. The topper was when Gillette told me I would now be receiving serious consideration as a World Series broadcaster. A thrilling moment for me.

But that decision would not be made until the season

ended. If New York and Brooklyn were the competing teams and Mel Allen and Vince Scully represented each franchise, that would eliminate any other Yankee or Dodger announcers and I'd be next in line. But would the Dodgers get in?

I was broadcasting the Senators while keeping tabs on National League scores. The tension increased day by day. Would the World Series opportunity come through? All I could do was wait.

And then finally the waiting was over. The Dodgers clinched the pennant on the last day of the season, and the choices were made: Allen and Scully from the competing teams, Bob Neal the network choice, and I was the sponsor's selection. There was the call from Ed Wilhelm, an executive with Maxon, Gillette's advertising agency, with the exciting news that my big chance had arrived. "Get to New York," Ed said, "we're all looking forward to having you with us." I could have flown there without a plane.

The broadcast would be heard coast-to-coast on the Mutual Broadcasting System, and around the world via the Armed Forces Radio Network.

I arrived in New York two days before the Series was to open at Ebbets Field on October 3rd, checked into the Warwick Hotel, and bought every one of the New York newspapers. Herb Heft, the publicity man from the Washington Senators, joined me in my room and we began preparing for the Series opener. I had hired Herb to join me to assist with notes, background information, and as statistician on the broadcasts.

There is only one way to prepare for a broadcasting event. Do your homework. I handle every big sports event as if it were an examination in college. My best assurance against nervousness is preparation. Not that nervousness can't be an asset. It

My weekly variety show, plus game broadcasts on WDNC (CBS in Durham, NC), helped pay my way through Duke University. Here with Duke football captain Bob Barnett.

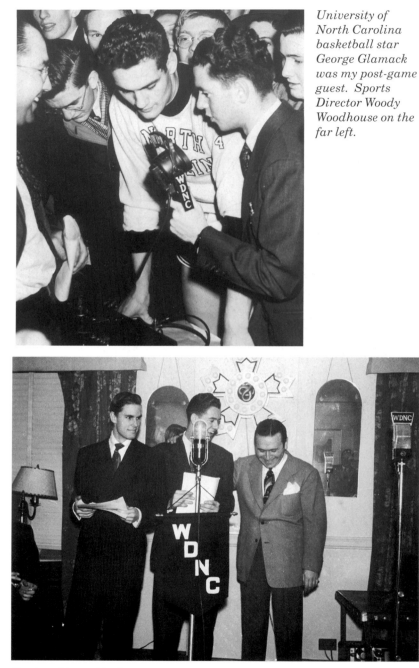

University of North Carolina basketball star George Glamack was my post-game guest. Sports Director Woody Woodhouse on the far left.

During Sigma Nu fraternity rush week at Duke University, Charlie Spivak and his orchestra were in town. We made him an honorary member in broadcast ceremonies at the frat house. Fraternity Commander Bob Anthoine was on my right, Charlie on the left.

Supply Officer with the 11th Special Stevedore Battalion in the Solomon Islands.

While still in the service, when my work at the Navy Department concluded late in the day, I'd journey to the Washington Post *radio station, WINX, to broadcast my nightly sports show.*

THE DAY in my life— MAY 5, 1945. Marriage in the Bethesda Naval Chapel to Navy Nurse Jane Louise Hoy.

Shortly after signing in 1946 as Washington's first telecaster, a variety show was added to my sports work. In keeping with our low budget, the show was entitled "Wolff at the Door."

The first sponsored TV show on DuMont, WTTG, in Washington. Barney Kraft, who owned the Southern Venetian Blind Co., had seen one of my pioneer shows and was willing to take a chance on this new medium. We inked the contract on TV.

Working out with the Senators in spring training each year (and pitching batting practice during the season) always helped the rookies' morale. "Hey, if that guy can make the club," I heard a newcomer say, "I can be a big-league star."

Shirley Povich, the famous Washington Post *sports columnist, was even listed in* Who's Who in American Women. *When Shirley received the publication's questionnaire, which included an inquiry about sex, his reply was "occasionally."*

My first coast-to-coast football partner—Al Helfer—on the Mutual Broadcasting System. An excellent broadcaster and good friend.

Behind owner Clark Griffith's desk were his pictures of presidential openers in the nation's capital. With a great ability to spot talent, the "old fox" kept the Washington franchise afloat without any corporate financial help.

Merry Christmas card—1954. From left, young Bob, Rick, Bob, Margy, and Jane in our Washington, DC, backyard.

Christmas greetings—1970. Same cast: Bob, Rick, Bob, Margy, Jane— now in Scarsdale, NY, 16 years later.

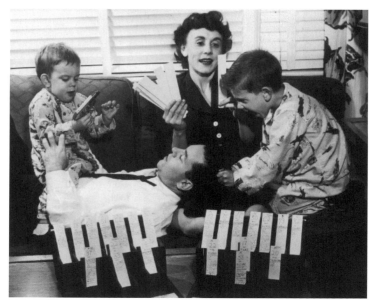

Memorizing football numbers did have a few distractions. That's Rick with the water pistol, Bob with the hair-pulling, and Jane helping me with my homework. Our baby Margy was sleeping.

With celebrated coach Vince Lombardi, guest speaker at the Con Edison Westchester Scholastic Sports Award Dinner.

With a champion—Joe Louis.

Another champion—Rocky Marciano.

An interesting Washington ensemble. Top left, pitcher Mickey McDermott, singer Eddie Fisher, shortstop Bob Kline, comedian Milton Berle, and outfielder Roy Sievers. Lower left, infielder Harmon Killebrew and myself.

Harry Howell Night at Madison Square Garden as the Ranger hockey great was honored in a soldout ceremony.

Visiting with former President Harry Truman. In DC, covering his throwing out of the first ball, the media guessing game was whether the ambidextrous President would throw righty or lefty.

I received cigar-smoking lessons and instructions on where to place the cigar in my mouth.

means your entire body is getting ready for the challenge. Once the game begins, it's replaced by intense concentration.

Herb and I went over all the material on the Dodgers and the Yankees. Three-by-five cards were filled out with all the information we could gather on the players. We had their basic statistics, their averages, an anecdote or two about each player, any fact or tidbit we could gather that would help me inform and entertain. How players were utilized during the season, what each pitcher threw, the relief men, types of hitters in the lineups, the platoon players, pinch hitters, lefties and righties, who were the speed merchants, the best arms, the basestealers —all the inside information that could add to the strategic flow of the game.

Brooklyn won the first two games in Ebbets Field. The Yankees came back to win the next two. The Series was now tied at two each. Game five was scheduled the next afternoon, October 8, 1956, in Yankee Stadium.

The Dodgers had won their first World Series ever in 1955 and now were trying to prove that their triumph was no fluke. The Yankees, embarrassed by the defeat, were being driven by their crafty old manager, Casey Stengel, to prove that 1955 was an accident.

We ordered dinner in our room at the Warwick and Herb and I looked up from our small, white cards for a break when it arrived. Don Larsen and Sal Maglie were the pitchers for the next day.

Larsen, 26 years old, had been 11-5 for the season. He had improved tremendously after a slow start when he switched from a full over-the-head windup to a no-windup motion. Casey Stengel had always liked Larsen as a pitcher and protected him when the freewheeling righthander had driven into a telephone pole in Florida early one spring training morning.

Maglie, 39 years old, a Dodger through a trade with Cleveland, was 13-5 for the season. He had been the tough Sal the Barber for the Giants, a Dodger-killer, before coming back to the National League with Brooklyn, a marvelous pickup who had pitched a no-hit, no-run game against the Phillies on September 25, 1956, in a must-win game for the Dodgers. Maglie was one of the oldest men in baseball history ever to record a no-hitter.

"Wouldn't it be something if Maglie pitched a no-hitter against the Yankees?" I said to Herb.

"Nobody pitches no-hitters in the World Series," he answered, and was right. Nobody had. In 53 years, there had never been a no-hitter in a World Series game.

I would set the scene for the fifth game with a 15-minute opening report. Bob Neal would do the first four and a half innings, and I would do the last four and a half.

The radio booth was in the mezzanine section of the stadium, directly behind home plate, with a fine view of the action.

Besides Neal and myself, Herb Heft was in the booth, along with engineers Giff Campbell and Ed King, executive Frank Zuzulo of Mutual, and Joel Nixon, our producer. Paul Jonas, who had been Mutual's sports director for many years, and Art Gleeson, who was now in that position, came by to wish us well. We were minutes away from the start of the fifth game of the 1956 World Series. The drama was about to unfurl. What a drama it would be.

At the end of three innings neither team had come up with a baserunner. Nothing but outs. During the commercial break, I talked to Joel Nixon.

"Pretty clean scorecard," I said, beckoning to the unsullied hit columns. "If it's still that way when I take over, the way I'd like to handle it is to keep informing everyone of exactly what's happening — there are countless ways and synonyms to describe how a pitcher has not yielded a hit — without using the specific words 'no-hitter.' Is that all right with you?"

"Fine," said Nixon. "As long as you make it clear."

Only three innings had gone by. It all seemed very academic. Nobody pitches no-hitters in World Series games.

During my years in Washington I had considered many times what my approach would be if the no-hit situation were ever to arise. Whether people should or should not be superstitious was hardly the question. The fact is that some were, and they were entitled to their rights as well as anyone else. If I could inform everyone without offending this group, I'd be fulfilling my broadcast role in the broadest possible manner.

But the key I knew was not just the choice of words — it was when they were used. A broadcaster, I felt, could make any reference he wanted to the no-hitter in progress, including the actual words "no-hitter" if he desired, as long as he avoided using them just before the pitch was made that could end it all. The pitching feat could be described as frequently as necessary, after each half inning, or after each out if need be, but antagonism arises if one juxtaposes the no-hit reminder just before the pitch is on the way. If there's a hit, the listener has every right to yell, "Why didn't he keep his big mouth shut?"

And why lose the impact of proclaiming the most dramatic words of all — "a no-hitter," "a perfect game" as the closing lines when synonyms along the way can inform just as well?

Mickey Mantle up. Two out. Bottom of the fourth inning. Here's Maglie's pitch to the Yankee center fielder...there's a high drive out to right field...it's going...it's going...that one's gone...a home run by Mickey Mantle and the Yankees lead, 1-0!

Mantle, a switch hitter, batting left-handed against Maglie, had hit a long flyball that landed half way up the first deck in right field for a Yankee lead. There was no question about the first hit of the game. It was tagged. Maglie got out of the rest of the inning without damage as the Dodgers came up to bat in the fifth. This was Neal's last half inning. I would begin broadcasting in the bottom of the fifth.

One out. Gil Hodges is up. Larsen ready, here's the pitch...a line drive to left-center field...Mantle racing over...racing over...he makes a back-handed catch...Mickey Mantle has robbed Hodges of a double, maybe more, with a brilliant back-handed catch of a line drive deep into left-center field!

Sandy Amoros went out and the Dodgers were down in the top of the fifth inning. Larsen still hadn't allowed a single base runner. He had retired 15 straight with the help of Mantle's fantastic catch. I was about to take over at the microphone.

Nine years before, in 1947, Red Barber had been broadcasting a World Series game between these same two teams. Bill Bevens hadn't allowed a hit through eight and two-third innings. The Yankee righthander then gave up a double off the wall to pinch hitter Cookie Lavagetto. The Dodgers not only broke up the no-hitter but won the fourth game of the Series with that blow. Barber had used the words "no-hitter" as the game went along. He had mentioned it just before Lavagetto doubled. Superstitious people blamed Barber — a most able and honest reporter. These cries might have been muted had there been a different word cushion between the no-hit reminder and Lavagetto's hit. I gave one final thought to synonyms and timing.

...and now to carry you through the rest of the game, here's Bob Wolff.

Chapter 14

The Perfect Game

Hi, everybody. It's not only a great game — but what pitching performances! Larsen has retired all 15 men he's faced; Maglie has given up the game's only hit and only run, the homer by Mantle. We move now into the bottom of the fifth.

The Yankees went out in the fifth and the Dodgers came up for the sixth. It was still 1-0 in favor of the Yankees and the Dodger fans in the crowd were pulling for a Brooklyn rally. Games were tied 2-2 and the Dodgers wanted this one to get ahead so they could win at Ebbets Field with a victory in the last two games. Carl Furillo, Roy Campanella, and Sal Maglie went out easily. The Yankees rallied again in the bottom of the sixth. Andy Carey started it with a single. Larsen bunted him to second.

Bauer is the batter against Maglie. The righthander delivers...a line drive to right field...base hit...Carey's coming around third and in to score as Furillo throws the ball to second base. The Yankees lead, 2-0.

Before the inning ended I mentioned that the crowd was becoming increasingly aware that the Yankees had supplied the only offense so far — two runs and four hits — while the Dodgers had been going down in order.

It's Not Who Won or Lost the Game—
It's How You Sold the Beer

No runs for the Dodgers in the top of the seventh. Larsen has retired 21 straight men. The Yankees have four hits. That's all there are in the game.

Now the crowd's response became part of the drama. They were restless through the Yankee seventh. They wanted the Dodgers to bat. They wanted to see Larsen pitch again. They wanted to see if such a feat were really possible. As soon as Jackie Robinson came to bat, the crowd grew still. They were no longer just rooting for a game. They were rooting for themselves to watch an historic game. I have always believed people root for no-hitters almost as much for their own part in it as witnesses as for the pitcher's part.

Jackie Robinson up, Larsen ready, the pitch...right back to the mound. Larsen has it, throws to Collins, one out. Here comes Gil Hodges. Outfield shaded toward left. Last time up, Hodges was out on a wicked line drive to left center in the fifth inning.

The crowd was more tense than ever. This was the man who had threatened Larsen the most. Hodges was an imposing figure at the plate, a big man, deep in the box, his cap pulled down well over his forehead.

Hodges swings...a line drive...right to Carey. Two out. Amoros up. Larsen looks in, gets the sign, delivers, Amoros swings, there's a flyball to center field, Mantle is there, under it...he has it. The Dodgers are out in the eighth inning with nothing across...and their totals remain blank in the ballgame. Larsen has retired 24 straight Dodgers as we await the final chapter. The Yankees have two runs, four hits, and no errors.

The Yankees couldn't go out fast enough in their half of the eighth inning. It was as if they were as anxious as the fans to see if Larsen could do it. Now it was the ninth inning. The scheduled hitters were Carl Furillo, Roy Campanella, and Maglie. There would certainly be a pinch hitter for Maglie.

Larsen was ready to pitch to Furillo. The pitcher took a deep breath and threw his last warm-up pitch. Now the Dodger right fielder dug in at home plate. The crowd was still. There was very little movement or sound anywhere.

Furillo, 34 years old, a Dodger for 11 seasons, kicked some dirt off his shoes, pumped his bat at Larsen, and looked out at the pitcher. Larsen bent low to study Yogi Berra's sign.

Now he's ready...the pitch...there's a foul back behind home plate...strike one.

The roar was intense...louder than anything in the previous inning. The crowd was in the game as much as Larsen. Emotions were running deep. Was there rooting for winning or losing or was there rooting only for the historical moment? Don Larsen was on the threshold.

The pitch...ball one.

Groans. Gasps. Some boos. Furillo removing more dirt from his shoes. Larsen standing on the rubber, a tall figure, bent over, his eyes on Berra's stubby fingers...one finger down...Larsen, a deep breath...

Furillo swings...a flyball to right field...not too deep...Bauer getting under it...has it...listen to that crowd...One question consumes them all...is it possible?...can it happen?...With one out Larsen goes to the resin bag...now looks in...here comes Campy.

The Dodger catcher, a stocky figure, moved slowly to the plate. He swung a heavy bat, dropped it, and picked up his regular bat. He was 34 years old and had been with the Dodgers since 1948. He had been playing professional baseball since 1936, starting in Philadelphia in the Negro Leagues as a 15-year-old. He had played with Josh Gibson, had caught Satchel

Paige, and was behind the plate in three different towns on the same day as a youngster. Growing old now, he had batted only .219 but had hit 20 home runs with 73 RBI. Campanella was still an outstanding hitter when he got his pitch.

Larsen looks in at Berra and gets the sign...now he's ready...rocks and delivers....there's a groundball to second... Billy Martin has it...over to first...Campanella is out. Two down...the crowd is going wild...the fans are yelling, shouting, cheering... what a moment...what a game!

Everybody was standing now with Dale Mitchell coming out of the on-deck circle to hit for Maglie. The Dodgers were down to their last out and they had called on Mitchell to pinch-hit.

"My job was to get on base any way I could," Mitchell would recall years later. "It was still a 2-0 game and if I could get on I could bring the tying run to the plate. I was just looking for a pitch I could handle."

Mitchell had hit .300 in six seasons for the Cleveland Indians. At 35, he had been an effective pinch hitter for the Dodgers. Now he was the man between Larsen and the greatest pitching feat in World Series history. Mitchell was a left-handed hitter standing 6'1," weighing 195 pounds, with a stance slightly bent over. He had faced Larsen many times before in the American League. The only thing different now was Larsen's no-windup style. That, and the 26 straight outs.

Mitchell steps in. Larsen's ready...the pitch...Larsen fires a fastball just off the plate...ball one.

Babe Pinelli was the home-plate umpire. He had announced before the Series that this would be his last year of umpiring. This would be the last time he would umpire a major league game behind home plate.

Larsen looks in...here's the pitch...a strike called...a

fastball...one and one the count on pinch hitter Dale Mitchell.

The crowd noise was deafening...a rising sound which reverberated through Yankee Stadium...all eyes were on Larsen, studying his every move, his back bent as he waited for Berra's sign...then suddenly the silence, the almost unbearable moment of suspense as the pitch was on its way.

Larsen throws...Mitchell swings and fouls it back...ninth inning...two out...two strikes, ball one to Mitchell.

Larsen took off his cap and rubbed his forehead. Now he put the cap back on and bent low again for the sign. Berra wiggled his stubby finger. Larsen began to pivot his body.

Here comes the pitch.

Babe Pinelli stood immobile at home plate. The baseball was in Berra's glove but there was no sign. Pinelli had waited a long instant. It seemed very long. It seemed as if all the world had suddenly been frozen in its place for that fraction of a second. And then Pinelli's right hand began moving up from his side, the fist clenched tightly, now at his head, now over his head, now stretched to its full reach.

Strike three called...a NO-HITTER...he's done it...a PERFECT GAME for Don Larsen...Yogi Berra runs out there, he leaps on Larsen...and he's swarmed by his teammates...listen to this crowd roar...Don Larsen has retired all 27 Dodger batters in a row. He has pitched a perfect no-hit, no-run game, and the Yankees win the fifth game of the Series, 2-0!

There were 64,519 people standing and shouting and waving and laughing. They had been part of history. As Larsen had completed his masterpiece, they were guaranteed a small piece of fame. They had been there. They had seen it with their own eyes. No one could ever take this game away from them.

I never realized how tense I was as I broadcast this game

to 60 million people until it was over. Then I couldn't lift my right arm. It ached for 24 hours. I had thrown every last pitch with Larsen.

Letters and telegrams poured in from people all over the country and throughout the world who told me how thrilled they were to listen to the broadcast and share in the emotion of this historic game. With all the kind words, I will probably remember best the man driving his car that afternoon in Idaho. He had lost control of his vehicle and crashed into a railroad car at a crossing. When the judge asked him what had happened, he said, "I wasn't concentrating on my driving, your honor. I was too busy listening to Bob Wolff describe Larsen's perfect game."

The case was dismissed.

Chapter 15

Playing Hardball

It was a can't-miss idea. I had agreed to make a guest appearance at the Landon School in Bethesda, Maryland, for their annual Father-Son Alumni softball game.

"Bob," came the telephone call from a father, "it would be great if you'd do a few innings of play-by-play on the public address mike — you know, introducing the fathers and sons with some build-up comments on their play. Make them sound big-league. It would be a real highlight for us if you'd say 'yes.' "

Sounded like fun to me. The school wasn't too far away, and I could work this in before leaving for that night's game at Griffith Stadium.

"Be glad to," I responded, "just send me a note with the time to be there, lineups if you have them, and a few notes on the players, and I'll add to them to make them all sound like supermen." Then I had an intriguing thought. "I have a great idea for you. I'll be with Harmon Killebrew earlier in the day. He's leading the league in home runs, you know. Why don't I ask Harmon to join me? The kids or dads won't recognize him in his regular clothes out of uniform. I'll introduce him as a father and bring him up as a pinch hitter sometime in the game. After Harmon swats one out and is trotting around the bases, I'll reveal his true identity, and the kids will love it. Would you like me to ask him?"

"Absolutely, that would be just fantastic. That would be really special if he would do that. Please let me know, and I'll keep it quiet, of course. We would all be thrilled. What a stunt to watch Harmon clout one — and then announce his name."

(Younger readers should understand that, in those days, players and broadcasters would participate in events such as these because they enjoyed doing so, and because of the pleasure it brought to others, particularly youngsters. There were no fees, no agents involved, it was just good will.)

"Sure," said Killebrew, "I'll be happy to go."

When we arrived at the school, there was a microphone set up at the side of home plate. I noted the short outfield, ringed by woods, and nobody took note of the gentleman by my side. Just another dad in sportscoat and tie who seemed more like a spectator than a player. A few hundred people were already on hand. Harmon took a seat away from the crowd, and, after checking the revised lineups, I was ready to begin.

A lot of laughs as I excitedly gave the game a tense championship sound, even extolling poor plays as "fantastic feats." Then the propitious moment arrived. Men on base, two outs, a tie game, just the spot for the unknown hero.

"And now folks, a pinch hitter for the father's team." I conjured up a fictitious name. Harmon took off his sports jacket, loosened his tie, and picked up a softball bat. There was no hum of recognition by either side, no murmurs from the spectators. So far the scheme was working perfectly.

Harmon stepped in, the first pitch was lobbed right down

the middle. Harmon watched it carefully, had it measured, uncorked a mighty swing, and barely tipped it.

This had to be a fluke, of course. I could visualize the next one being swatted, not into the trees, but over them. Just throw the pitch.

In it came — as big as a watermelon — Harmon waited — there was that beautiful home run cut. Strike two. Nothing but air.

Everyone was silent. I began to perspire. "C'mon, Harmon," I muttered to myself. "Just tag one. Please."

I saw Harmon brace himself; I felt confident again. This had to be the one. There was the pitch — Harmon cranked up, let loose — Strike three swinging.

Now what do I say? What do I do?

"Wow," came out the word, "just tipped that one. Another swing coming." No one seemed to take notice. Just another father up there trying to make good.

The reprieve brought about a dribbler back to the pitcher, and Harmon was an easy out.

It was confession time. "Well, fans, I've got a big surprise for you. The man you've just seen at bat is not one of the fathers; no, it's the great Harmon Killebrew, who undoubtedly will become one of the most feared home-run hitters of all time."

I continued, "Harmon, would you give the fans a demonstration of your might?" Now everyone perked up. And Harmon went back to the plate and proceeded to continue his futile flailing — pop ups, grounders — the ball didn't leave the infield.

Now the hole's getting even deeper. The natives are getting restless. They want the game to go on.

So I finally say, "Harmon, why don't you just fungo one out yourself?"

They give him the ball and he swings at this elusive object, managing to hit some line drives and a couple of hard groundballs, but he never gets under one to really lift it up in the air.

The gimmick has run its course, and I say, "Harmon is always a great sport, fans, and he doesn't want to break up the game by losing your softball. So let's give him a hand."

There was polite applause and pretty soon we got out of there.

Poor Harmon. All the way back I had to console him. "Don't worry," I remember telling him, "you hit a hardball real well. This is just a different sport." And he nodded his head.

Harmon went on to hit 573 home runs in the big leagues, and only four guys ever hit more, Henry Aaron, Babe Ruth, Willie Mays, and Frank Robinson. Harmon capped his productive career by election to the Baseball Hall of Fame, a richly deserved honor.

But I can kid Harmon about that game at the Landon School over 40 years ago. I remember telling him that someday he was going to make the Baseball Hall of Fame, but added with a smile, "that will be for hardball, of course." Harmon just laughed. He's my kind of guy.

Chapter 16

The Phone Call

With the Washington Senators, in addition to broadcasting the games, I was also the host-interviewer on all their surrounding pre- and post-game TV and radio shows. National assignments were now coming my way as well. Then suddenly, piercing this foundation of good fortune, was a telephone call prior to my nightly show — a call which continues to perplex me. It's a secret that I've kept till now, but I believe that time has erased what was then a most vexing problem.

The call, unexpectedly, was the first and only one I ever received from Mrs. Clark Griffith, the owner's wife.

"Bob, Clark and I enjoy listening to you so much and watching you on TV. You've been a good friend of the Griffiths. And now, here's a chance to do something for you. Here's a story for you — a scoop that should help you. Bucky Harris will be returning to Washington to manage the Senators again. That's it — there's the story. It's yours."

Startled? Absolutely. Pleased? Yes — at the generosity of doing this for me. But worried? And how. Was Mrs. Griffith representing Mr. Griffith in this? It had to be. He had to be able to say that he personally hadn't told me. That must be the reason.

"Gosh, thanks, Mrs. Griffith. That's awfully nice of you to call me with the story. The Griffiths have been mighty good to me and I truly appreciate it."

We exchanged a few more pleasantries and I hung up. I had that eerie feeling that I must have been dreaming. Was this real? Was this really a thank-you present so that I could scoop the town? But maybe I should hold the story back in deference to my colleagues. If I did, though, would the Griffiths think I wasn't being grateful? I certainly couldn't call Mr. Griffith and ask him what I should do with his wife's story.

Airtime was approaching. I checked the wires — no indication of any announcement. I was on the air in half an hour and still pondering what to do. I finally decided to go with it. I revealed that Bucky Harris would be returning to manage the Senators.

But before I did so, I passed the favor on. I called Paul Jonas, the sports director of the Mutual Broadcasting System, who had given me my first network radio exposure.

"Paul, here's one for you. I know you have a sports show coming up soon. In about 10 minutes, I'll be breaking the story that Bucky Harris is returning to the Senators as their next manager. It's yours to use, too." He was most appreciative.

"Sorry, Paul, I can't give you my source, but it's a most reliable one. Go with it."

The story, attributed to me, was carried on all the wire services, coast-to-coast.

The next morning my phone was ringing early. "Mr. Griffith wants to see you. How soon can you get to the stadium?" I said give me an hour, and I was on my way, puzzled as to what was next in store.

When I arrived sports columnist Shirley Povich of the *Washington Post* and sports columnist Francis Stann of the *Evening Star* were waiting in Mr. Griffith's office as well. I quickly noticed that no one was smiling.

"Bob, that's a terrible thing you did," Mr. Griffith exclaimed, "both to the ballclub and to these men and their readers. You killed our biggest off-season story by breaking it in advance. How could you do this to us?"

I searched his face frantically, looking for any subtle expression which would let me know he understood why. Was he just pretending innocence, or did Mrs. Griffith reveal something in her desire to help me that was their household confidence, but without her husband's knowledge? The thought was a chilling one.

"What's your explanation?"

I could not tell the truth. I could not confide how I got the story. If I lost my job, at least I'd go down with honor.

All eyes were riveted on me. "What do you have to say?"

"When I broadcast and telecast the games," I said, "I try to be honest and fair; but I do recognize that I represent the team, and would not hold that position without the club's permission. I want the Senators to succeed on the ballfield and at the box office, and I do my very best to fulfill your expectations in every way.

"All of you are my personal friends, and that friendship is more important to me than breaking any story on the air that was being held up for print coverage.

"You have never told me what to say or what not to say. I don't need a guide for that. I follow a simple rule. My own sense of what's right and what's wrong. I want to help you, and not hurt you. That's the way I live my life. I'm not hungry for scoops or sensationalism. I'm far more concerned with my honor as a person.

"I do have other obligations, however. I do have nightly TV and radio shows away from the ballpark. Those stations expect me to be a good reporter, a journalist, to search out stories and report them. This story came to me before my nightly radio broadcast. It was from a reliable source, and I used it as a news item, just as if it came from the Associated Press. I did not speak as a spokesman for the club.

"Your feelings mean a lot more to me than a couple of lines on the airwaves. I'll be glad to say tonight that this is an unconfirmed report. Obviously, it's not an official announcement unless you declare it to be so.

"I did not want to detract from any forthcoming announcement of a story which still may be in the works. Henceforth, I will check with you Mr. Griffith if I ever pick up a story about your ballclub that I believe will involve you personally before I put it on the air. I cannot and will not reveal my source, but I'd like to consider this matter closed. I've learned a lesson."

I left the room, still baffled. How embarrassing it would have been to have checked with Mr. Griffith on a story which came from his house. Was this a game the "Old Fox" was playing, making me contrite when he knew the source of my information? Was I the scapegoat in an acted drama, or did Mrs. Griffith, in an effort to bestow a favor, take this strictly into her own hands, without regard to the household consequences and the print reaction?

In all my further years with the club I never revealed to Mr. Griffith, or his son Calvin, or Shirley, or Francis, or anyone else in baseball, what had taken place.

I did call my mom and dad, though, along with Jane. They're the most ethical people I knew. My parents lived every day to be good to others, to be positive, to bestow praise when it was due, to measure one's life achievements in good deeds bestowed on others. I try every day to follow their example.

I needed their reassurance, and I received it.

I never told the story.

But now, Mr. Griffith and his lovely wife, Addie, are in Heaven, hopefully organizing a Hall-of-Famers' team in that league on high. They're a great couple, and this story, in retrospect, may bring them both a smile. I certainly hope so.

If they think I handled this well on Earth, and am still one of their favorites, I'd like them to consider me as one of the future broadcasters for Griff's heavenly team. And I promise not to reveal the story in advance if I'm the one selected.

Chapter 17

Space Race

Television money brought about big changes in ice hockey during the 20 years I did Ranger broadcasts. Increased TV coverage meant more income. Expansion fees came about as more cities joined the league. More cities meant a better chance for network exposure. For the players it meant more job opportunities and more bidding for services. The gold rush was on.

Almost all the early players were from Canada, and the Montreal and Toronto teams latched on to them. Having played in junior leagues in Canada, they were all known to the Canadiens and Maple Leafs. Hockey Night in Canada was a broadcast tradition, and Foster Hewitt, the broadcaster, was a household name.

On February 28, 1960, I teamed with Hewitt to provide from Madison Square Garden the first pay-TV event in hockey history, sent to a movie theater in Canada. There was talk then that pay-TV would be the next big development in TV revenue. Over 30 years later, except for a few special events, they're still waiting to hit the jackpot.

Hockey is an easy sport to describe on TV or radio, but only if you know the players well, or have the numbers memorized.

The number method is difficult as they're placed only on the backs and sleeves of uniforms. If you're sitting at mid-ice, and the players are skating toward you, numbers don't help. You have to wait till they go by to get a better angle.

If the booths are high up in the arena, hairlines were an important identifying sign, until helmets obscured that possibility.

If you're with the same team over a few weeks, players become recognized easily by body movements and skating mannerisms, but if a sportscaster is starting a new season without a training camp behind him, it's imperative to learn faces and numbers. In the season's overlap, with baseball ending and hockey about to begin, preparation demands some cram sessions.

Phil Watson was the Rangers' coach. I was commuting from Washington to New York, going by taxi from the airport right to the Garden and the Rangers' dressing room. There I focused on each player's features up close, silently mouthing his name. I'd look from one to the other, simulating a quick play-by-play under my breath.

I followed this procedure for the first three games, before doing the play-by-play. After those unobtrusive sessions, I could make quick calls on the air. Facial recognition along with size, shape, and style made numbers less important.

When I was set to enter the Rangers' dressing room prior to game four for one last run-through, the trainer Frank Paice stopped me. "Sorry, Bob, no more," Paice said, blocking my entrance.

"No more what, Frank."

"No more coming in here before the game."

"Why not Frank?"

"No more, that's all."

"But Frank, please explain why."

"Well, Bob I'm just passing on the word from the coach, Phil Watson. You know what happened the last three games, don't you?"

"No, Frank, what happened?"

"We lost — that's what happened."

"Well, Frank, if that's the problem, tell Phil that before I started the Rangers' season I was in the Yankees' locker room during the World Series. They won. I also was in the winning locker room at the NIT, the Gator Bowl, well it's a long list, so it's just possible that my being in the locker room can help the Rangers win. Tell Phil I'll come in a bit earlier next time and make sure to impart my special magic. If Phil needs help, tell him I can be his secret weapon. Let me know."

I waited, Paice left and then returned. "Sorry, Bob, Phil just can't take a chance."

A couple of weeks later, with the Rangers still struggling, my plane from Washington to New York was late arriving at LaGuardia. It was a race against time. Already sweating, I didn't want to lug my traveling bag upstairs to the overhang TV booth.

Racing by the Rangers' dressing room, I heard the crowd roaring and realized the Rangers were already on the ice warming up.

A quick decision. I ran back to the Rangers' room, opened the door — only the clubhouse man was there — left my bag just inside the trainer's room and motored upstairs.

Getting to the booth on time was a close call, but one that

my nerves had become accustomed to in order to fit Washington broadcasts and Garden events into my daily schedule.

On this night the Rangers won a tight one, and the Garden was rocking. That made for a happy post-game dressing room.

I closed the TV show, and, with no post-game restrictions from Phil Watson, went down to chat with the players. In the middle of the media gathering, I spotted Frank Paice.

"Frank," I said, "here's the proof I was telling you about a couple of week ago. Here's my bag — right here — in your room —up against the locker. Now let me tell you something, Frank. I put it there before the game on the way up to the TV booth. So understand this, Frank. I was in this room before the game and the Rangers won. Please explain that to Phil, and see what he says now."

When I arrived at the Garden for the next game, there was a message that Frank Paice wanted to see me.

"Yes, Frank, what is it?"

"Well, here's what Phil would like to do. He would appreciate your coming by before the next game and leaving your bag in the room. Of course, Phil would then want you to leave! But he would like your bag in the room. What do you say? Can Phil count on you?"

I laughed, and told Frank I'd make it available on future overnight trips to New York, but I couldn't promise it for the next game. The Rangers won that one, the urgency was gone, and I retired the bag undefeated.

With a full fall TV and radio schedule in Washington, along with all the events at Madison Square Garden, and weekend college and pro football around the country, I seemed to be up in the air more than on the ground.

My daughter, Margy, then three years old, used to sum it up pretty well. She looked up at airplanes and called them "bye-bye-daddies."

So it was welcome news when I heard one day that the Rangers were coming to Washington. The reason — a fund-raising exhibition game against the minor league Washington Hockey Lions at Uline Arena to benefit a talented young sportswriter, Carroll Hall. He had lost sight in one eye when a puck came whistling over the sideboards while he was covering a practice session at the ice rink.

I told the Lions I'd do my best to help them and the Rangers and came up with a plan to cut down on charity expenses.

"Great thing you're doing," I told Rangers Traveling Secretary Pat Doyle. "Here's what I can do to help out. I'll arrange to have a big bus meet you at the railroad station, furnish a tour guide — my secretary, Shirley Sager — and give the team a quick look at the nation's capital. Then you'll all be brought to my house. I'll supply the dinner for everyone. The bus will then bring you to Uline's and, after the game, take you back to the railroad station.

"You'll have no worries, nor any expenses for Washington transportation, lodging, or meals and that can help the fund."

The Rangers gave me an immediate okay, and now the work began.

First the bus. When I explained the cause to Trailways, they told me they'd supply one without charge including the driver.

Home was a four bedroom Cape Cod, two-and-a-half baths, with a small finished basement, and a backyard framed by Rock Creek Park. It was situated on a cul-de-sac in the northwest section of the city. This was our first home after a cramped apartment existence, and though it looked large at the time, on later return visits to the city, it seemed to shrink at each viewing.

It was great for a small family, but not exactly suited to housing a 30-man Rangers' entourage, along with Jane, three children, a bus driver, a secretary, and the Washington media who wanted to meet the team.

The time had come for the most important part of the transaction — to discuss this planned event with my wife.

"Jane, I've invited some friends for dinner on Friday. I hope that's okay with you."

"That's fine. Who are they?"

"The New York Rangers hockey team."

"The what?"

"The Rangers hockey team."

"You're speaking about a few players, of course."

"No, not exactly. I mean the whole team, starters, reserves, staff, media, about 30 or so."

After the shock wore off, Jane suggested a catering service, and we carefully checked our bank account before splurging for filet mignons, potatoes, vegetables, salads, desserts, beverages, and shrimp platters to begin this midday feast. The catering crew was dressed formally for this gala occasion, adding an extra element of festivity.

The guided tour was a great success, and all was in readiness for lunch when the huge Trailways bus arrived at our small home — a rather incongruous sight.

Only one hitch developed, but it added a certain charm to the day. After lunch, the players, according to their routine, wanted to nap before leaving for the arena.

The search began for floor space.

Twenty players played musical chairs for one king-sized bed, and three smaller ones. Two curled up in bathtubs, others used the living-room floor, the den, the kitchen, the hallways, the backyard — bodies covered every inch of space. Walking through, over, and around them was an agility-testing experience.

Then it was back on the bus to drive to the game, a Ranger win, incidentally, with a nice boost for Carroll Hall, and then to the railroad station.

Jane was her usual effervescent self as the hostess on that memorable day, but I've never surprised her again with "by the way, I've invited a few friends for dinner."

Chapter 18

Personal Items

Fifty bucks a week was a major investment for me at that early time in my career, but a couple of New York friends assured me this would be my springboard to fame and fortune.

"You've got to be better known in New York to get the big New York assignments," said one, "and that means getting your name in the paper. You can't do that while spending so much time behind a mike in Washington, so you have to hire somebody who'll make you a daily New York column item."

"Do you know such a person?"

"Absolutely. Artie Pine is your man."

I called on Artie some weeks later. He had a small Manhattan office, bare walls, two desks, and a telephone. On one desk was a typewriter, on the other a pile of clippings.

"Trust me," Artie said. "Favorable items — you'll be pleased with them. A little humor, no controversy. Just keep feeding me what you're up to — names, dates, and places, and I'll do the rest.

"We've got seven papers here in New York, and there's *Variety*, *Billboard*, and all the trades, plus the wire services. People will know all about you — a great door-opener for jobs.

"Just jot down your upcoming schedule, leave me a bio, and I'm ready to begin. I'll send you clippings every week."

And within a week I was in the big time, nestled in column notes along with the celebrities, the stars, the Broadway favorites.

Most of the entries were one-liners, quoting Wuff, or Woof, or Wolf, or Woolf, or Woolffe, or even Wolff, at a speaking engagement, or a fan club appearance, or a ballgame, or while lunching with network executives, or discussing a contemplated new show with eager producers. It appeared that I was moving around the city pretty well. Did I really have a fan club? Was Artie it?

The "humor" lines would never bring any creative or comedy writing awards — some I couldn't figure out — but somehow they were in print. Was there an old joke book hidden away in Artie Pine's office, or did he just make this stuff up on the way to work? Amazingly, it was printed.

Sometimes I was referred to by the columnist as "my good friend, Bob." One stranger even called me "talented." That was nice.

These bon mots were usually spoken at hotels or restaurants I had never heard of, or occasionally in a conversation with some budding actor or actress I had never seen.

I figured these were all three-for-one deals for Artie, getting paid by the eatery and the fledgling thespian along with myself.

I wondered how he pulled this stuff off. Maybe he ran an exchange program feeding columnists like Ed Sullivan and Leonard Lyons some really hot items each week about entertainment stars and, in return, they'd throw in the Wolff note as part of the deal like "the player to be named later." Or maybe they just liked Artie.

I had to do some belt-tightening in those days to afford this New York publicity bonanza, but began to realize only my vanity was being fed — no new jobs arose to justify the expenditure.

Reluctantly, I bowed out after a few months, denying readers my newest witticisms, but only after congratulating Artie for delivering all those print mentions. I thanked him and hoped that someday our paths might cross again.

Some years later, while I was at Madison Square Garden, I received a call from Joe DiMona, my old friend from Washington DuMont days, whose expertise on the perils of pouring hot beer had avoided a potential sponsor's problem in the TV booth.

After graduating from law school, Joe passed the bar (friends say it was the only bar Joe ever passed) and was now thriving as a writer in New York.

"Big news, Bob. Let's have lunch. I've got to tell you all about it.

"I just made a fortune," Joe announced at our get-together. "I'm going to make a half million dollars or so on my newest book, *Last Man At Arlington*.

"I found the top literary agent in New York," Joe confided, "and he put the book up for bids. There was great interest. And we retained the movie rights — that'll bring in a lot more. Bob, I've hit the jackpot. It's thrilling."

"That's terrific, Joe. I'm so pleased for you. All that hard work in the writing game really paid off. And I'm sure glad you found the right literary agent to make it work. That's another plus for you."

"Yeah, I got the best. Terrific guy, too. I'd like you to meet him someday."

"I'd enjoy that, Joe. What's his name?"

"Artie Pine. I'm sure you don't know him but he's tops in his field. I know he'll enjoy meeting you, too."

By way of celebration, Joe sent each of the Knicks a copy of his book. He asked me to hand them out in the locker room, a little heavier read than the usual post-game stat sheets.

A few years later, Joe struck pay dirt again. His H.R. Haldeman book, *The Ends of Power*, was a national bestseller. And Artie Pine was now dealing with by-liners instead of one-liners.

Chapter 19

Switching Teams

In the '50s I never asked how much a ballplayer made. Figured it was none of my business. Nor did they know my pay structure. I'm sure we all shared a common thought — that we were underpaid, but it was difficult to find a way to measure this. Today, salaries are as well publicized as batting averages, and reported as part of the story.

Washington's Roy Sievers told me that after a terrific season, leading the league with 42 homers, a .301 batting average, and a league-leading 114 RBI, he had enough impressive credentials to ask for an increase. Certainly worth a try. So Roy made an appointment with the club president to discuss his situation.

Mr. Griffith listened patiently as Roy presented statistical proof that he obviously should earn more.

"I'd like to do it, Roy," came Mr. Griffith's answer, "but we just don't have the money."

That's a tough statement to counter, but Roy gave it a valiant try with an impassioned plea about his value to the club.

Roy says he'll never forget Mr Griffith's closing words. "Roy, we lost with you, and we can lose without you." That ended it. They continued to lose with him.

I was fortunate in year-end accounting that I got paid separately for every show I did in addition to broadcasting the ballgames. There was a fee for each pre- and post-game radio show, and another for each pre- and post-game TV show. The radio shows were taped and played against the live TV appearances. I received an additional check for ownership of the TV shows as I presented a complete package to the station or sponsors. The package included the cost of my cameraman, assistant producer, the technical work on the program, and my fee for airwork and production.

In 1961 George Weiss asked me if I would consider being the New York Mets' announcer. He was acquainted with my work as he could hear my Washington radio broadcasts at night, and he had seen me on Madison Square Garden events. The first question he posed to me was how much would it take to bring me to New York.

I told him it would be exciting to return to the city where I was born, but I couldn't give him a definite figure until I knew the extent of my duties. He asked how much I made in Washington and, when I told him, he said that was more than the New York City baseball broadcasters. I pointed out that no New York announcer also owned and broadcast all the shows adjoining the games as well as broadcasting the games themselves. We decided to speak further.

That same year the Senators moved to Minnesota, became the Twins, and I joined them as their broadcaster in this new venture. I continued my nightly radio show to Washington via telephone, commuted to New York to do Madison Square Garden events, and did weekend assignments for the ABC-TV network, hosting their college and pro scoreboard shows. A new baseball franchise had gotten underway in Washington, and their trainer was Tom McKenna, who had held that post with the Minneapolis Millers. We made a "house trade" for the summer. He moved into our Washington home, and I took his, moving there from a hotel as soon as school was out and my family could join me for the summer.

When the season ended, stories began to appear in the New York, Minneapolis, St. Paul, and Washington papers as well as *The Sporting News* that I might be leaving to join the new franchise in New York which was opening in 1962. The Minnesota Twins' sponsor, Hamm's Beer, became increasingly restive as speculation increased, particularly because they felt the local townsfolk might infer that leaving would be because I didn't enjoy their area. They offered me a longer contract and a raise, and urged me to sign up quickly so there was no doubt about my feelings.

I spoke to George Weiss and told him that, if he wanted to continue discussions with me, it would have to be done quickly, as the Minnesota people were pressing me for an answer.

His reply: "Bob, I like your work, and believe you can be an asset to our team. We have one sponsor lined up — Rheingold Beer. I'd like you to meet the brewery heads and their ad agency as soon as possible, but we're also trying to get an additional sponsor and are still negotiating with a TV station to carry the games. I'm going to recommend you, but I'd feel better if the others could share in the final announcement. Can you hold off a few more weeks on the Minnesota deal?"

As it happened, I was selected as the 1961 World Series broadcaster and told Hamm's I'd have to be in New York and Cincinnati for the next two weeks, but after that I'd be free to come to Minneapolis and talk. By return telegram, they set a date for our meeting, and said it would embarrass them to wait any longer than that. Applications for my job were already piling up, and the papers were writing that I was leaving them.

When the Series ended, rather quickly at that, in five games with the Yankees winning, I spoke to George Weiss again, and was asked to wait just a little longer. "George," I said, "I'd be thrilled to come back to New York all year round. I'm doing network shows there. I have a home in Washington, spent the summer in Minnesota, and the rest of the time in airplanes. The people in Minnesota have treated me very well and I can't keep them waiting indefinitely. I promised them an answer this week, and I have to live up to that. I thank you for your personal interest, but have to withdraw from your broadcast consideration. Maybe sometime in the future it will work out."

I flew to Minnesota with my business manager Milt Fenster, signed a new contract with Hamm's, and looked forward to a new season.

Then came the unexpected. About a month or so later, the Mets finally completed both a contract with a TV station and their sponsor lineup. It was now time for their announcer selection. Their first signing was Lindsey Nelson, followed by Bob Murphy and Ralph Kiner, an outstanding trio.

The twist to the story is that Lindsey had to leave his post as the NBC-TV Game-of-the-Week announcer to join the Mets. NBC then offered me his job to join Joe Garagiola on the network. Milt Fenster and Tom Gallery, the NBC sports director, worked out the contract. I'd do coast-to-coast games every weekend, and would be stationed in New York where I could do other network events as well. All this providing I could get a release from my Hamm's contract, and if I would leave my studio shows and play-by-play calling on ABC-TV.

ABC-TV consented to release me and I flew to Minneapolis for another consultation with Calvin Griffith, the Twin's president, and with the Hamm's people.

"Gentleman," I said, "you know that I have shown good faith by withdrawing from New York Mets consideration and signing with you. Now I am asking you for a favor. If I had joined another club, people here might rightfully ask why I'd leave the Twins to go to some other team. The NBC Network is not some other team. In fact, Twins games will be on their schedule. This contract allows me to attain something that every baseball sportscaster prizes — network status. But more important, for the first time in my career, by doing network games just on the weekends, it gives me a chance to spend more time with my family and I'm asking you to give me that opportunity."

They suggested that I step out of the room while they talked it over, then they beckoned me back in. "Bob, you understand our feelings. We're proud of our area, you've seen what a great place it is, and our commercials reflect that pride. For you to go to another team would be a slap in the face. This is the place to be for good living. But the network is another story. It does give you a chance to spend more time at home and we understand that and respect your feelings.

"We're also pleased that NBC confirms our judgment of your work. So we're giving you permission to withdraw from your contract and do so with one stipulation. It's this. We'll call the press conference and issue the press release. That release will explain that we're proud that you've been selected for this new assignment, but you're leaving with our permission and approval because it gives you more time to spend with your family. Hamm's believes in that. We'll add, of course, how much we both enjoyed our association. This will be announced on TV, radio, and in the papers in our words."

I said that would be just great, gave up my summer home in Minnesota, sold my home in Washington, and moved the family to New York to accept my new position. Sometimes a detour proves to be the best road to take.

Chapter 20

Suggestion Box

It was a high-level meeting at NBC-TV. That means there was something at stake — hopefully, not the announcers. Ratings is always a sure-fire topic, and on the way to jousting with the big chiefs, I started thinking along those lines.

Joe Garagiola and I were competing on Saturdays and Sundays with the rival CBS-TV "Game-of-the-Week," pitted against Dizzy Dean and Pee Wee Reese.

The contrasts jumped right out of the TV set at the viewers. Joe and I concentrated on trying to be accurate, informative, and entertaining. Preparation was intense as we spun from city to city. I kept updating player information, Joe kept adding to his wealth of stories and humorous one-liners, keeping his material fresh and timely. The former big-league catcher had great insight on the game and was a master of proper timing. My job was to impart the excitement of the play-by-play, clear the way for Joe's comments, and make sure our blend conveyed the enthusiasm of two guys sitting together and enjoying every moment of the game and its subtleties. This was a pleasant but delicate exercise we both worked at diligently.

After a while it became second nature — a true partnership. We each learned how our roles could synchronize. And after each game we would discuss our comments and our timing. Joe could unerringly recall what he had said almost pitch by pitch, his concentration on words was that intense. There was no upstaging. We worked as a team, and I prized our relationship.

Joe was and is a quick-witted, funny guy — a major force in sports humor. That's a rare gift and he set the standard.

On the airwaves, Joe and I were getting excellent ratings in the cities and more cosmopolitan areas. A lot of our banter had a word base to it — quick lines, fast thoughts, unusual similies, and rapid exchanges. The emphasis was always on baseball, though, and the strategies and nuances of the game.

Our competitors on CBS took a completely different path, and their personalities and approach made their style work in a different manner.

Dizzy Dean was a large ol' country boy with a big grin, a cowboy hat, booming voice, and a devil-may-care style. He had a captivating "hello pardner" greeting for everyone. Diz rarely knew names and that included the ballplayers he described in his game broadcasts. This didn't concern Diz. He never bothered to keep a scorecard, had no notes, no worry about statistics, words, cues, or any broadcast formalities. His irreverence was intriguing, though. Diz butchered the language, had the PTA writing petitions to get him off the air, made up his own words like he "slud" into third, and when he got too bored with the proceedings, burst into song and talked about life on the farm.

Diz was a character, a personality, and delightful company. He kidded me about my "book larnin" and I poked fun at his "syntax." Diz thought that was some tax placed on immorality. One couldn't kid about his pitching, though. Diz was a great one.

To give the CBS telecasts a semblance of real baseball, Pee Wee Reese, a Hall-of-Famer in his own right, did a straight play-by-play during his innings on the air, and Gene Kirby, a solid baseball man and broadcaster, kept a scorecard for Diz and either whispered to him or gave him notes on what was happening on the field.

On Saturdays and Sundays, NBC and CBS opposed each other. Two different styles, different games, but each vying for the televiewers' attention.

The inner-circle meetings usually start the same way. A lot of back-patting. Opening lines usually include "everything going great," and "viewers love you."

This is like batting practice, sort of a warm-up drill, while the pitcher is getting set for the game. This is the time for circumventing the issues, but giving out disguised hints which subtly lead to conclusions. This is the art of never being the villain, utilized in disclaiming any criticism which could backfire at some later date. It could be termed fencing, pulling punches, shadow boxing — but it's easily recognizable by all in attendance.

Finally, down to the heart of the matter, presented to me in a delicate manner.

"Bob, you and Joe are doing a terrific job. You're both true journalists — accurate, enlightening — the games are exciting — they're enjoyable in every way. In fact, they're so good, we can't understand why we shouldn't be winning the ratings battle in every section of the country. We're ahead in the cities, but not in the farmlands. We have the talent to make it a complete victory.

"We just can't believe that there are some folks who seem to enjoy that clowning that goes on at CBS. Maybe people tune in to laugh at them. Maybe some fans feel superior when they hear all the mistakes they make, and the mispronunciations, and not knowing the players — it's a travesty — very bad — we all feel the same way — it's not baseball broadcasting, that's for sure —but it does draw some viewers — those guys up in the hills, I guess, who don't want any part of this educated stuff.

"So we've been thinking. Why don't we fight fire with fire? Maybe we should beat them at their own game and sweep the ratings all over. People laugh at mistakes, at being goofy. It shows the announcers are human — announcers shouldn't mind incorrect words now and then — or not knowing all the answers. Who really cares about the rules all the time. Being human and fooling around could bring in more viewers, you know. Not that you're not perfect now, of course, this is just a thought about fattening up ratings all over the place. Just a thought, of course. Maybe we're just too good."

Now the spotlight was on me. Response time.

"Gentlemen, I'm delighted you called me into this meeting. I completely understand your feelings. You've put a lot of thought into this, and that's why this network is so successful. We work together, but our fields are different. My field is reporting, yours is selling. Selling is your specialty, and I understand big ratings make that easier for you.

"Now, I can understand the suggestion you have made — it's the execution that presents a great obstacle. Let me explain. I've spent years of preparation in high school, in college, and then as a big-league broadcaster learning how to be accurate, prepared, and knowledgeable in baseball. One major reason why I was hired to do three World Series and the NBC "Game-of-the-Week" is because I've trained myself as a journalist. That's the image I've built up through a lot of hard work. I don't wear my Phi Beta Kappa key, but I take great pride in the reputation I've made as a broadcaster who's always prepared, and literate too. Proper word use has helped me tremendously in my career, not just in baseball, but in all sports.

"It would take me years to learn how to discard all my accuracy habits and start making mistakes. Of course, this could be done in time. I could forgo all preparation for games, write down 10 or 15 names to mispronounce every game, and, of course, laugh at this on the air, and I could sing, too. I enjoy singing, but as I said, it might take years before I got the knack of acting like a fool.

"Of course, we might gain an audience of dropouts, but think of all the present viewers who would tune us out.

"But, what the heck, if you insist on this, let's call a press conference and announce this change in the NBC-TV style, that we'll try to be unprepared, with mistakes and inaccuracies. The press and the public should know we're doing this just to please them by descending to a lower level. I can help out by having my PR man call the major columnists to advise them of this change of policy — I know we'll get plenty of ink.

"Now, because my illiteracy may be an instant hit, obviously I can no longer go back to my old style and image. The public will now view me in a different manner — as will advertisers. Therefore to protect the network which obviously will have a great new attraction, so that they don't lose me, I think a new long-term contract would be a necessity, in fact, a must.

I'm sure the network could use me on their other comedy shows, too. That's long-term value. So what do you say? When do you want to announce this, and when should my business manager come by to negotiate?"

There was silence in the room.

And then. "Just a thought, Bob, nothing serious, of course. Nothing that has to be discussed again — outside this room. We just wanted you to come in and meet the fellows, so we could repeat what a great job you and Joe are doing. Keep up the good work."

I thanked them for their confidence in the telecasts and left. The idea was never broached again.

Just another day in the TV business. When the "Dead End" sign appeared, the time had come to get back on the original road.

Chapter 21

Punch Lines

MICKEY McDERMOTT was a happy-go-lucky, fun-loving pitcher when I first knew him as a stylish southpaw with the Senators. Among his later stops was the New York Yankees, and it was in New York that I saw him again in a post-game locker room celebration at Yankee Stadium after a Yankees' Old-Timers' Day.

"How've you been doing, Mick? Gee, it's great to see you again." I had a microphone in my left hand, and my right hand forward for a handshake.

Looking at the TV camera I confided, "Mickey was a fine pitcher. He had the talent to be a league leader had he wanted to."

"Yeah, in booze and broads," he chortled, and I knew that Mickey had aged, but hadn't changed.

"I led the league in stolen towels," he continued, showing the same devilish humor that had made him a favorite personality years ago.

It's interesting to discover but sometimes embarrassing to find out what some of these elder statesmen are now doing, but I gambled.

"Mickey, what are you doing these days?"

"I'm doing nothing. I'm a millionaire."

I laughed. "Still the same old storyteller, eh Mickey?"

"No story, I'm a millionaire — that's the truth."

"Mick, I know you too well. You're speaking to Bob Wolff, Mick. Remember I know your stories, but the public will be hearing this too. This is on TV."

"I'm telling you the truth. My wife hit the lottery. Seven million dollars. Ted Williams called me. He said 'Bush, good for you. Enjoy yourself.' "

"Okay, Mick," sounds great, but Mick...."

"I'm not kidding," Mickey roared. "Mickey McDermott — a millionaire. I've got my limousine waiting outside."

❖ ❖ ❖

My TV cameraman zeroed in on HECTOR LOPEZ as I taped an interview with the former Yankee infielder at Yankee Stadium.

Knowing we already had two previous long interviews on the same tape, I got a little concerned after we had spoken about 10 minutes or so. Feeling the tape might run out, I said a quick goodbye and then, just to make sure we had the whole Lopez interview, turned aside to my cameraman. "We got all of that, didn't we?"

"Well, not really, just the first few minutes."

"Just the beginning — how about the rest of it? It ran about 10 minutes. What happened?"

"The tape ran out."

"I sort of gathered that, but why didn't you tell me when that happened?"

"I guess I could have, but I didn't want to interrupt you in the middle of your interview."

Sometimes, you can only laugh.

❖ ❖ ❖

ARTIE SUSSKIND was a most valuable behind-the-scenes man at Madison Square Garden events, assisting with the television coverage. On some events, he dug up pertinent notes for my use in the TV booth.

I televised the entire spectrum of Garden offerings with one exception.

I refrained from covering wrestling — although I recognized that these acrobatic actors had excellent athletic ability and were adept at inciting reactions, either as heroes or villains. Even as theatrical presentations, repeated slammings to the mat never seemed to be a fun way to make a living.

Artie had a role at the TV matches, though. He was there at ringside, right next to the grunt and groaners and was responsible for the show ending right on time in the allotted two-hour period.

His signal to bring the final match to a rousing crescendo of tumult and triumph was raising both arms over his head. This somehow inspired one of the gladiators in the ring to come up with a breathtaking pin, bringing the roar of the crowd to its highest level as the show concluded on time.

One night, Artie, feeling a little tired, yawned, and inadvertently raised both arms over his head.

The startled wrestlers, who had barely worked up a sweat, knew there was no deviance from the cue.

Wham — bam — it was all over — in almost wrestling-record time.

The TV station was in shock. Twenty minutes to fill. What to do? A hasty conference — then both wrestlers were called back into the ring for post-match interviews — somehow another fight developed — which, as you may have surmised was settled before the hour struck.

The crowd loved it, a novel ending, a great finale, but Artie's ring survival was in jeopardy. He received a warning —with yawns, stretching or otherwise, arms had to be kept pinned at his side. There could be no further confusion as to when to be up in arms. Artie promised to comply — and the shows continued to end on time.

❖ ❖ ❖

TRACY AUSTIN was playing a tennis match at Madison Square Garden that started late and ran even later. Following long baseline duels, in and out of deuce, we moved into the early morning hours with the end not yet in sight.

Every 30 minutes I was asked to say on Channel 11, "Please stay tuned to watch 'The Prisoner of Cell Block H' immediately following the tennis."

After the fifth entreaty to stay tuned to watch "The Prisoner" right after the match concluded, I felt it was only fair to add a warning. "Please stay tuned to watch 'The Prisoner of Cell Block H' if he's not out on parole by then."

❖ ❖ ❖

I hired MAURY POVICH as an assistant while he was still in high school. Talented, energetic, he enjoyed the zest of competition on the field and off. Maury worked with me as my

110

statistician on baseball, and in a wide variety of jobs on my other TV shows. A creative young guy, with my small staff, he had his pick of titles.

When the Senators moved to Minnesota, Maury came with me as my right-hand man. I felt he also provided insurance, being able to step into the play-by-play role if I couldn't get from the TV to the radio broadcasting booth in time or vice versa. I did innings on both media.

One day in Detroit, the game was running late, and I had to make a plane connection to New York for a network show.

"Maury," I whispered, "here's your chance. I'll finish up with the next batter, then I've got to run. You can take over, can't you?"

"Absolutely," Maury answered, his eyes gleaming with this first major league opportunity.

And in a matter of minutes, Maury had his big opportunity —he was calling a Harmon Killebrew home run.

His description was excellent, but just as memorable was his comment. "That's the longest home run I've ever called," Maury exulted on the airwaves.

No one can deny that statement.

❖❖❖

My behind-the-scenes statistical and production staff during the Washington Senator days was comprised of young, talented high schoolers or collegians. I hired kids who were eager and smart and knew their stuff in sports. Sportswise secretaries augmented the team, and made sure that our large schedule of TV shows fulfilled our expectations.

How young were my booth assistants? Well, Maury Povich

was in his teens when he joined me. Earlier, high schooler DICK HELLER, now a popular sports columnist for the *Washington Times*, assisted me with stats and notes in the TV booth as did youngster PHIL HOCHBERG, now a prominent Washington attorney.

Phil still laughs about the day he arrived at my home, ready to go to the ballpark with me, too young at the time to drive there himself.

Our good friend, Eleanor Wood, was with Jane, and answered Phil's knock at the door.

"Is Bob here?" Phil asked.

"Not yet, but he should be home from school any moment now," Eleanor answered. "I'm sure he'd enjoy playing with you. Why don't you come in and wait!"

Phil was faced with explaining that he was not young Bob's playmate, but actually his father's right-hand man — or at least a teenage equivalent. A bit later we left for the ballpark together.

Youth must be served, the saying goes, and I got a lot of good breaks from those who took an early chance with me. My young assistants justified my faith in them, and all played an important role in the success of the telecasts.

P.S. Incidentally, there were no TV veterans in those early days. We were all pioneers.

Chapter 22

Acting Natural

I prize words — admire good writers and applaud their artistry. It takes talent to race the deadline clock while pouring out a well-crafted story combining informative content and readership appeal.

Broadcasters get a break in their on-air coverage. Immediacy makes the job easier. And their emotional response in reporting the story can be more important than the words they use in the impact on viewers and listeners. Wow! Oh, baby! Unbelievable!

Writing has to come after the emotional moment. Broadcasters give vent to their feelings as they happen.

Broadcasters don't have to worry about choosing the precise words at the crucial moment. They just have to open their mouths and let their excitement erupt. The words are secondary to their feelings.

Most highlight broadcast calls are made by local broadcasters, uninhibited in their hometown glee as their voices rise in exultation on the airwaves. Network broadcasters have to exert a more disciplined approach. They realize that unrestrained cries of joy cause animosity from dejected losers, and the network broadcasts to both sides. Network calls still reflect emotion but the broadcaster has to remain objective, eliminating any local rooting bias.

Just by nature, I happen to be an emotional person. I believe this helps in my work. I don't have to act — when I act natural. It's just the way I am.

Sportscasting is not for the shy or inhibited. As one's voice is raised to convey excitement, animated people would seem to have the edge. They just have to be themselves. Crowd roar provides a stimulant, but without it, the sportscaster provides his own emotion. There's no crowd roar in the studio, however. Yet the highlights are provided at a higher pitch with simulated emotion.

Acting natural when others are looking or listening is an art that can be acquired, but one has to act — natural.

Emotion is expressed through the rise and fall of the voice and through the choice of words. Although the words should just pour out in emotional moments, pure and unscripted, it is vital to maintain a mental check on what's being expressed. The words remain long after the emotion has subsided.

TV or radio sportscasting is not journalism in the traditional sense. Sportscasting is live theater. Content is vital to hold interest, but, unlike writing, the words are just part of the picture. The sportscaster deals in the transmission of thoughts through a variety of methods — a raised eyebrow, a smile, an inflection, an excited voice, an emotional call, a pause — they all can have far more impact than the limitations of words. That's unfortunate for anyone who prizes proper grammar, and the use of synonyms to enhance descriptions — but it's true. There are few mikemen who work diligently at producing the precise word to fit the situation.

Yes, there are story lines, observations, game notes, and play-by-play descriptions. However, journalism, usually thought of as newspaper coverage, relies on the use of words to paint a picture. Sportscasting — TV or radio — uses emotion as its base. Sometimes just the picture tells the story.

Sportscasting requires acting ability. Providing vocal excitement at the microphone is a necessity. The better sportscasters are skilled in the use of many dramatic finesses not required by the writing press. They use voice levels to induce moods, and raise or lower their voices backed by the roar of the crowd. And if they're doing a studio highlight sports show without any crowd roar, sportscasters raise their voices anyhow, bringing their own excitement to the video. On camera, the sportscaster can induce moods with smiles or frowns.

Most newspaper game stories capture the essential details of an event. They reflect craftsmanship through an on-target assemblage of nouns, verbs, adjectives, adverbs, thoughts, and phrases, hoping to create a complete visualization for the reader. Writers strive for an easy-to-read but compelling style that informs, enlightens, and appeals. Stories can have an emotional base, but lack of immediacy can lessen the impact on the following day. A broadcast, taped and played following the game, never is as fulfilling as hearing and viewing it while it happens. Live broadcasts have the emotional edge.

The great TV and radio calls of our times rarely have a literary foundation. In fact, it's not what the sportscaster has to say, it's how he reveals his personal excitement that has the impact on the listener or viewer. The sportscaster becomes the participant in the event — he's shouting "Unbelievable" into the mike just like the guy at home who's shouting this at his television set.

Memorable TV and radio calls, in fact, are usually stripped to the bare essentials. Played over and over again on highlight films, records, and tapes, their stirring quality relives the feelings of the historic moment.

Proof? Listen to the actual words used in some of sports' most replayed calls:

Bobby Thomson's Home Run (Russ Hodges) "THE GIANTS WIN THE PENNANT! THE GIANTS WIN THE PENNANT! THE GIANTS WIN THE PENNANT! THE GIANTS WIN THE PENNANT!" The unrestrained feeling is what counts.

1958 Colts-Giants NFL Championship (Bob Wolff) "THE COLTS ARE THE CHAMPIONS! AMECHE SCORES!" The words are like headlines. No embroidery needed. They're right to the point. In this call, I realized after I heard the playback that I shouted the winning team first and then the touchdown maker. That's the most important progression. During a game the scorer comes first, but emotion dictated that this time the Colts, not the player, became the first verbal headline.

Don Larsen's Perfect World Series Game (Bob Wolff) "STRIKE THREE CALLED... A NO-HITTER!...HE'S DONE IT...A PERFECT GAME FOR DON LARSEN...YOGI BERRA RUNS OUT THERE, HE LEAPS ON LARSEN...AND HE'S SWARMED BY HIS TEAMMATES...LISTEN TO THIS CROWD ROAR!" The perfect words — "a no-hitter," "a perfect game" need no embellishment. The roar of the crowd provides emotional accompaniment.

USA's Olympic Hockey victory over USSR (Al Michaels) "DO YOU BELIEVE IN MIRACLES? YES!" Right to the point. A precise question and summation. An emotional exclamation point.

Boston Celtics NBA Eastern Championship over the Phila-

delphia 76ers (Johnny Most) "HAVLICEK STOLE THE BALL... HAVLICEK STOLE THE BALL... HAVLICEK STOLE THE BALL... HAVLICEK STOLE THE BALL..." Pure emotion — the repetition of the four key words that preserved the Boston win.

Neither embellishment nor variety are necessary with the spoken emotional word. For brevity, Marv Albert, who has brought his unique cadence to sportscasting by utilizing short staccato phrases in quick powerful audio jabs, has compressed emotion and reporting into one word..."YES." Kids in the schoolyard can sing this out when they hit a basket.

Mel Allen stayed at the top in baseball calls with three words. Homers, regardless of height, distance, or location were broadcast as "going, going, gone." The favorable response to his famous trademark call never changed. Description could come later. I tried not to invade Mel's proven staked-out territory by making each of my calls as unique as the homer itself, while realizing that few remember descriptive words as much as emotion.

John Madden's exuberance and informed comments zoomed him to the top spot among football analysts. With arms flailing, his voice rising, his genuine passion for his sport grips viewers and listeners who are swept up by his enthusiasm. He charges into the broadcast booth much like fired-up college players bolt out of the locker room. Emotion is the key.

This is accentuated even more because he is paired with a low-key and most effective calm partner in Pat Summerall. It's an unusual switch of roles, teaming a restrained play-by-play caller with a high voltage analyst, but they pioneered this most successfully.

Can you imagine two loud announcers together or two

subdued sportscasters as partners? There'd be no balance. Proper pairings are important.

Dick Vitale, the basketball whiz, has become a national personality with his revved-up vocalizing. He's the ultimate cheerleader, breathless, ecstatic, making each move seem so meaningful that the viewer can't afford to turn away. His playground phrases of unrestrained glee have made him a vibrant figure, imitated and respected. Is it a great act — or is it emotional response? Regardless, Vitale's emotion sounds natural and that's why it succeeds.

John Davidson, the hockey kingpin, knows that one fervent "oh, baby" doesn't need any more literary polishing. Successful Dick Enberg believes he can satisfy the rank-and-file, along with the erudite, by proclaiming "oh my" at the crucial junction. This is not my personal favorite as it seems more suitable for a ladies' tea than a ballgame, but Dick's popularity with those words remains high.

Hockey announcers vie for who can shout with more feeling the traditional "he shoots, he scores." These oft-repeated words can be exclaimed with such fervor that no more description is necessary, nor does anyone seem to be concerned about the lack of variety in this tried-and-true standardized call. Hockey could use some new descriptive words, however. Writers work at synonyms. Few sportscasters do, but is the need there?

And how about the "gooooooooal" call by soccer announcer Andres Cantor that made him a World Cup celebrity. One long agonizing wail, like that of a wounded cow, gave him world-wide recognition. A repeated emotional call was his ticket to fame.

Sportscaster Warner Wolf, like most other sportscasters, gets transformed into an emotional state when he sits in front of the microphone. Warner's use of "let's go to the videotape" enabled him to hit the jackpot in Washington and New York television and on the ABC-TV network before completing a round trip back to the nation's capital. Warner keeps his energy up without changing the words. One heard "Boom" on every home run — five or six a night — and "Swish" on every made basket. That never changed, but why should it? Warner demonstrated that it's not variety of words, but emotion that matters, and when Warner enters the studio, he's got plenty of that.

Emotion unleashes a vocal accompaniment to drama, but there are hazards in its use. Faked hysteria, becoming more prevalent in the desire to command attention, sounds like what it is — contrived, insincere, and an unadulterated bid for attention.

Whipping up hometown frenzy has become a marketing tool used by many public address announcers to create a rock-concert atmosphere at ballparks and arenas. Fans are implored to "make noise, yell louder, scream, clap, charge" in order to inspire "our" or "your" team. The fan is led to fantasize that his or her participation has a bearing on the outcome of the game. The message board, buttressed by audio accompaniment, is there to spell out the commands. Marketed emotion.

Yet this is precisely the wrong direction for baseball to take. Baseball is a slow cerebral game, not a revved-up high action sport. It demands time to discuss game situations with accompanying family or friends without the blare of music or the noise of scoreboards threatening conversation.

Little kids know which team to root for without scoreboard guidance. Club owners have to understand that the beauty of the game they're selling is in its pacing, its tranquility, punctuated by artistic performances, climactic moments, and situations which evolve slowly and then build to a moment of high tension demanding intense concentration. The fan in the stands has to be given time to breathe, to talk, and, above all, to think, to muse, to contemplate, to imagine, to speculate, and to provide his or her own emotional response without the artificial contrivances designed to thwart these rights and make the spectators nothing but robots.

We've also seen that out-of-control emotion at the ballpark, sometimes escalated by alcohol or drugs, can mean serious trouble for players and fans. Everybody knows how to win, but learning how to cope with losing is vital.

Some players use emotion in a despicable way — to rid themselves of sportsmanship while taunting or insulting opponents, or even deliberately injuring them, condoned by some club owners who should be expelled from sports. Another misuse of emotion is that used by "homer" sportscasters who never concede that the local team has lost a game because the opposition played better. These moaners always have an excuse. "We wuz robbed," is their alibi, defeated once again by "incompetent officials," or "unlucky breaks." Sportsmanship has been wiped out of their consciences as they spew out their vitriol to their listeners. This is misguided emotion and biased reporting at the lowest level. The opponent never wins in their broadcasts, the home team has the game taken away.

And then there are those helmet-throwing, water-cooler-bashing childish ballplayers whose temper tantrums make a mockery of the self-discipline required for a sport where only the best ballplayers can hit safely three times out of 10.

So emotion can be tricky business. It's available to all, however. When used wisely, it enhances viewing and listening and becomes an essential part of the sportscasting business.

When used to make a ballgame a war or an opponent not worthy of respect, emotion can be a destructive force.

Sportswriting may demand more creative leads, more well-crafted game stories, a better word sense, and a more artistic literary approach, but reaction to the emotion of broadcast calls proves that vocal excitement has a great impact, an importance of its own.

The written word usually has long-lasting effect and reaction; the spoken word has immediate response, but except for some highlight calls, a shorter life.

A sportscaster who can combine lyrical words and vocal music has a good chance of going to the top of the class.

❖ ❖ ❖

I said goodbye to a good friend early Wednesday morning (May 1, 1996). It was not a sad occasion, but a frustrating one — as my friend, a baseball record — finally succumbed at just 34 years of age.

For the last few years, I knew the end was in sight, but I was powerless to do anything about it. It was a terminal baseball illness. Unfortunately, it's also contagious, spreading throughout the sport.

I was the TV broadcaster of the previous longest nine-inning game ever played — on NBC-TV coast-to-coast in 1962 when the Dodgers defeated the Giants, 8-7, in the playoffs in four hours and 18 minutes.

On Tuesday night (April 30th), the Yankees and Orioles played to a 13-10 Yankee victory that went four hours and 21 minutes, the new record, just 10 days after the Orioles had played a four hour and 15 minute game. As you may have noticed, four-hour games are becoming increasingly common.

Baseball was a different game in 1962, and should not be judged by present standards.

How different is today's game? Well, for starters, consider this. The game was limited in 1962 to a one-minute commercial after each half inning. Today, commercial time has more than doubled, and occasionally tripled.

Twenty-four or more extra minutes are now allowed per game — the #1 reason why games today are so much longer.

And how about playing time? Do you remember when pitching was considered 80 percent of the game? It's now a hitter's game, which is why softball scores abound. More hitting means more runs and longer games.

It's a rarity when a starting pitcher finishes a game. Too many middle relievers help provide relief to the opposition. Expansion has been their ticket to the majors.

Why is pitching so poor? Well, one explanation is the radar gun. Speed counts.

Bypassed are those who have mastered the art of pitching and winning. Atlanta with Greg Maddux and Tommy Glavine has proved that top-flight pitching can depend on finesse, not velocity.

In saying goodbye to my old record, which symbolized another era of baseball, I can only hope that it will rest in peace. But unless commercial time is shortened, and better pitchers are signed, the present time record will soon rest not in peace, but in pieces, and a day or night at the ballpark will mean exactly that. So bring a meal and a sleeping bag. Add an asterisk to the old mark to signify less commercial time — or perhaps add a dollar sign to the new record.

(Aired on SPORTSCHANNEL, NY, May 3, 1996)

Chapter 23

Animal Kingdom

No matter how you spell my name, it makes no difference on the airwaves. All spellings sound the same.

But in print, or registration, certificates, airline reservations, hotel bookings, restaurant charges, letters, phone bills, award plaques, newspaper columns, diplomas, TV fonts, and the like — the confusion that exists with Wolff is something to howl about.

Almost cost me a career.

Tom Gallery, the NBC-TV sports director, told me I should wait in my hotel room for his call — that it was important I go over cues and network notes with him prior to my playoff telecast from the Los Angeles ballpark.

I promised Tom I wouldn't budge till I heard from him and suggested we ride out early together to beat the game traffic. We settled on a time.

It was an afternoon game and to make sure there'd be no slipups, I set my alarm clock, left an early wake-up call, ordered early room service in advance, and awaited Tom's ring.

I read the morning paper for possible notes, and when the appointed time came, checked all the material in my briefcase, and stood up, ready to leave my room.

But no call. I began to worry.

Pre-game preparation is vital to a good telecast. Speaking to each manager, checking the lineups, talking with players, going over each team's press notes, and then readying the scorecard with the batting order, positions, uniform numbers and batting averages, homers and RBI starts the routine. Then comes diagraming each team's defensive alignment, listing the left- and right-handed hitters, switch hitters, lefty and righty pitchers to anticipate managerial strategies, and putting down quotes, compiled in the dugouts or at the batting practice cage that might be used in the game. All this plus going over cues and getting set for the opening on-camera appearance means taking time and care prior to the game. There's no short cut to preparation, and it's essential to doing the job right.

I called Tom's room. No answer. I began to sweat. I called the restaurant. Not there. I had him paged in the lobby. No response. That was it. No time to wait. I had to move — quickly.

I gathered up my notes, strode to the elevator, dashed through the lobby, and searched outside for the NBC limo and driver. Nowhere in sight. No cab, either.

Finally, one came by. I jumped in, closed the door, and with apprehension asked a vital question, "Do you know how to get to the Dodger Stadium at Chavez Ravine?" There'd be an awful lot of coast-to-coast dead airtime if we got lost.

The driver's "yes" was not reassuring, but I had to gamble. "Get me there as quickly as possible and I'll double your tip, but if you get lost, pull over quickly and get directions." My life or death — broadcast style — was at stake.

My shirt was beginning to feel damp. I was no longer

thinking about what to say on the telecast — I was just consumed with getting there on time.

Traffic was building as we approached Chavez Ravine. A taxi would not get priority. No press pass on the windshield. I kept looking for a police car. Maybe a friendly policeman could help blaze a trail.

I realized that, once we were inside the complex, getting to the Press Gate presented another problem. The driver would not know which turn to take in these sprawling areas. I anguished over how pampered I'd been by being driven there on press buses, or by NBC limo drivers who had directions in advance.

My forehead was wet, my tie undone. What had happened to Tom Gallery? Why hadn't he called? Why hadn't he left a message? Had I misunderstood the directions?

Finally, I arrived. I felt like I had played a full game myself. I paid the cabbie, added a grateful and bountiful tip, and made a quick decision. I decided to go right to the field to start my preparation rather than climb to the TV booth to check in. No time for that. But if Tom Gallery were in the booth —waiting for me — going frantic — would he already be lining up a replacement announcer?

"Think positive" I kept telling myself. Concentrate on game preparation.

Finally satisfied that I was prepared with lineup and notes, I made it up to the TV booth where I was met by my red-faced boss who left no doubt as to where I stood. "This is your last broadcast for NBC," Gallery bellowed. "Your last. When I give you orders to stay in your room till I call, I mean it. You're through after this one. I'll have more to say to you after the game."

"But Tom," I began.

"I don't want to hear it — get ready for the game. I'll speak to you later."

Just as well. I had to get that sinking feeling out of my mind, and psych myself back into a happy state — upbeat, enthusiastic, excited to be there. It was almost like self-hypnosis to be positive, but my mind had to come through, and dispel the negative.

And it did, to whatever strain to my body. To be a top-flight broadcaster, concentration has to be intense. Other thoughts can't be allowed to intrude.

Any lapse in the thought process can result in stumbles, mistakes, a glitch in the natural flow of words. There's a rhythm to the broadcast when it's a smooth one — any intruding personal thought can jam on the vocal brakes and stop the flow.

But my concentration held up — the game ended — I was proud of my effort — and limp with exhaustion from the inner battle to stay focused. I was relieved and smiling. But not for long.

Tom Gallery entered the booth. "Step outside, Bob." I followed him.

His rage returned. "That's never going to happen to me again. I'll hire someone who can follow directions. I can't believe you would do that to me."

"Tom," I interrupted as the veins started to bulge in his forehead and his face became beet red, "I never budged from my room. I finally called yours and you were gone. I couldn't wait any longer and grabbed a cab so I could get here to prepare."

"Bob, I called your room at least five times, had you paged, and there was no answer. Where were you?"

"In my room, Tom. What room were you calling?"

"How do I know. I asked the operator to ring your room."

"Okay. Tom, I have a pretty good hunch as to what happened. When we get back to the hotel, I believe I'll be able to prove to it to you. Until then, let's not discuss it. We're both upset. At least the telecast went well, and I'm thankful for that."

It was a tough ride back to the hotel. I couldn't wait to speak to the desk clerk.

"Tom, please come here beside me and listen to this." I spoke to the clerk. "Please call Bob Wolff for me and let me know whether he's in his room."

The clerk did so and came back.

"No answer," he said.

"Fine. Now this is important. What room did you call?"

"Room 960."

"And how is it registered?"

"Bob Wolf, *Milwaukee Journal*."

Gallery was taking this all in.

"Do you have another Bob Wolff here?"

"Another? I'll check."

"Why, yes we do. Came in last night with the NBC-TV group. I'm not sure it's posted yet by our operator, but I'll make sure it's done."

"What's the room number of the NBC Bob Wolff?"

"He's in room 580. Shall I ring?"

"No. I don't think that will be necessary."

I turned to Tom. "Tom, I never left my room as per your instructions. I even had breakfast room service there which you can check on the bill. Tom, you were calling the wrong Bob Wolff."

I smiled. "Tom, I believe you now understand what

happened. I was exactly where you told me to be. No apology is needed, of course, but you can now rehire me to continue doing your games."

Tom chuckled, put his arm around my shoulder, and said, "You're my man, you know that. Of course, you'll be with me. I hope you never thought otherwise."

Other wolves will attest there are two sides of this name-spelling story. As the years have gone by and the correct spelling of my name has become more prevalent, the scales have balanced, unfortunately, with the incorrect spelling of many of my colleagues' names.

In 1994, the Basketball Hall of Fame, in its newsletter, printed an obituary of player agent Bob Woolf, an outstanding sports lawyer who represented many of the country's top sports stars, including Larry Bird and Joe Montana. This loving tribute to a giant in his field was accompanied by a photo. The photo was of me.

Condolences came in, and passersby would do double-takes before taking a longer look, checking whether I was an apparition or the real thing. It was sort of scary to watch their puzzled expressions.

One person followed me for a further check. I couldn't resist telling him, "Don't be concerned — you're just watching me on replay."

Chapter 24

Fit to Be Tied

A few years ago I won 10 million dollars. That's what the headline said on the packet of magazine material I received in the mail. Now I know how Mickey McDermott felt.

I double-checked it, you can be sure. Ten million — all mine. It said so on the envelope.

It appeared that all I had to do to collect my fortune was to fill out a few enclosed papers, and if I liked — no one said it was mandatory — I might wish to subscribe to 20 or so of the large collection of magazines that made my award possible. They listed the magazines to make this easier.

Should be no problem there. I could just take the subscription money out of the hefty award that was coming my way. But they wanted me to subscribe now — the award wouldn't be coming for a while.

Of course, I had no time or inclination to read their magazines. Maybe I should just neglect subscribing and tell them to send me my winning check. That's what I did. Would they think that was fair — taking their millions without subscribing? My wife thought I was wasting a stamp by replying at all.

I guess something went wrong somewhere because I never

did win the jackpot — or any other prize — but I guess they still thought well of me, for some time later I received another letter — this time I had won 20 million, double the previous amount.

"Throw it away," said my wife.

"But, Jane," I began.

"Forget it. You haven't got a chance to win it, and besides, we don't need any magazines."

"But."

"There's the wastebasket."

A lot of my mail isn't that exciting, but I try to answer it, scribbling my responses en route from South Nyack, New York, to the News 12 TV studio at Woodbury, Long Island, where I have them typed.

My wife, who seems to have a photographic memory of the universe, does the driving — about 50 miles each way — and has never encountered a detour she can't surmount. En route in addition to the letter writing, I read the newspapers, listen to the sports news on the radio, start writing my 5:30 P.M. script, make phone calls from the car, and, with arms full, eat peanut butter and jelly sandwiches she's prepared along with apple slices.

One day, in turning the newspaper pages, a big glob of peanut butter and jelly made a splash — landing right on my tie —an unexpected mishap that would be most noticeable on camera.

I wiped it off; the stain remained though, and after Jane dropped me off she went in search of a new necktie that would blend with my suit. That accomplished, she brought me the new tie and then started her 50-mile trip home.

She would again make the 100-mile round trip later that

night in time to watch my 10:30 show, offer her critique (I was always sure of a good review there), and then drive us both home.

We both have always believed that everything happens for the best, but how messing up my tie would accomplish that was hard to imagine. I offered weakly, "Well, maybe a new tie might be more attractive, and if the stain comes out, I'll have an extra tie."

Some weeks later, I received one of those follow-up phone calls — you know the type — "Have you read our letter and do you plan to reply?"

"What letter are you speaking about?"

"The letter that told you we were giving away $40,000 and you're in line to win a prize, but you have to let us know you want to claim it by filling out the forms."

"You're kind to call, but the chances are I threw that away. After reading those million dollar payoff offers that the magazine companies put out, my wife and I decided we'd just throw this stuff away, and I guess that's what I did with yours."

"I can understand that, but this is different. You have until three this afternoon to sign your name to our forms, have it witnessed at the bank, fax the forms to us, and then we can send you a check. If you don't do this, though, your money goes back in the jackpot."

I was wide awake now. "Do you mind explaining this a bit more? How many magazines do I have to buy?"

"Not a one. You're already a winner. The charge card company you belong to has a bonus for lucky number winners. That number is the purchase amount that you made on your charge card on a specific day at a specific time.

"All who hit that number on that date and time will share

in the prize money. The jackpot is now $40,000. Your share will depend on how many on our computers hit the same number at the same time."

The spokeslady was from the firm that ran the contest. She faxed me the form. I rushed to the bank, filled out the blanks, had my signature notarized, had the material faxed to the spokeslady, and went back to the TV station.

About a week later, the check came in the mail — $680.

Curiosity got the best of me. I called the spokeslady and asked what the number was that made me a winner?

She took a moment and had the answer. She gave me the date and said the amount on my charge card was $70.20.

I called home and spoke to Jane. She was thrilled to hear about our windfall of $680.

"Did I make a purchase of $70.20 last month," I said.

"Yes, you did," she said. "Actually, I made the purchase for you — a new tie. The old one had peanut butter and jelly on it, remember?"

As we said — everything happens for the best.

Chapter 25

Legends

Modern-day listeners or viewers may not have heard of Bill Stern or Ted Husing, but back in the 1930s, '40s, and early '50s these two men were sportscasting idols, revered throughout the land. They were the voices of radio college football — Stern on NBC, Husing on CBS.

Television did not take hold until the mid-'50s. When that occurred, mellifluous voices were not enough — they had to be fortified with content, analysis, and personality. Voices would add to the game, but the video provided description. Golden tones were no longer considered as vital as before.

Bill Stern had a dramatic timbre to his voice that would have made him one of the world's greatest actors. In some ways he was an actor. Bill was often so transfixed by his own calls and stories that he would become overwhelmed with his emotional intensity. Tears would well up in his eyes as he spoke of on-the-field bravery and courage and athletic heroes worthy of our rapt attention.

I was going to Duke at the time, and was active as an undergraduate on local CBS radio, broadcasting college games, and conducting sports shows. Sometime in the future, I might be thinking of network glory, but, at that time, I was exulting in my role on local radio.

On a trip home at vacation time, my dad asked me if I'd like to meet Bill Stern and talk to him about my future in the field. Dad explained that a friend of his was a school chum of Stern's and had volunteered to arrange an appointment for me with the noted broadcaster.

"You never know," Dad's friend told him. "This is just the boost young Bob might need to get to the next rung."

And so it was set up, and there I was, person to person, with the best-known football sportscaster in the country.

We chatted pleasantly about Duke, and then about Bill's ability to play off the crowd roar, injecting extra excitement into his broadcasts. I had noted that, in turning from one station to the next, NBC always sounded as if its games were the most exciting. Bill admitted that keeping the crowd roar audio at a constant high level was by design. It worked, too.

He also told me that, on a fourth-down try that may or not have picked up first-down yardage, he'd tell the audience to listen to the sound of the crowd. The home crowd's cheer or groan would provide the answer — a little audio trick that kept the audience in the game.

When the talk turned to my future possibilities, his voice became a little more paternal.

"Bob," he said, measuring his words, "you're broadcasting now and having fun; that's the way it should be. Just enjoy it, and then put it behind you and use your college education to move into a good business opportunity.

"I can understand you may visualize yourself as the next Bill Stern, but the odds against that happening are so great —

millions to one — and you've got to be so lucky even to get the chance, it's just not worth the gamble.

"There are too many uncertainties in the business — too many people you have to please — too many out to get you — only a few ever get to the top — and then you've got to hold on or they'll cut you down. My advice is to do something else where there are better odds to succeed."

We chatted about his coming Rose Bowl broadcast, then I thanked him for his time and advice and left.

Frankly, I never gave heed to his words. I was a confident kid, too young to worry about my next step, and, after all, I had just met and talked to Bill Stern. The fact that he had given me a standard adult line "forget about it" didn't daunt me at all.

But when the friend of Dad's who had arranged the appointment called me and asked how the meeting had gone, he first became indignant and then enraged when I repeated the conversation to him.

"That's horrible," he said, "just horrible. You're off to a great start. You should be encouraged to continue, not discouraged. I can't believe he'd be like that — and I'm going to tell him."

"Please don't do that. What Bill Stern said doesn't set me back at all. Maybe he's right. Getting to the top can be tough, I guess. I appreciated his seeing me. That was a big thrill — just by itself. I'm not discouraged. I'm still enthusiastic, and, who knows, someday, he may change his outlook."

That someday came just a few years later after I began my full-time professional career in Washington. After every NBC football game, Bill Stern would close by saying, "And now stay tuned to Bob Wolff for the Camel Scoreboard." I had been chosen by the sponsor to follow Bill Stern on the network, giving scores and highlights coast-to-coast.

In addition to his play-by-play, Bill Stern had a weekly feature telling his famous stories. These stories were so implausible that the network was finally forced to preface them with a disclaimer, "These stories are based on hearsay." One of the most intriguing was about the first baseman about to be released after a batted ball hit a pebble and bounced by him.

As I recall this wild tale, the first baseman, distraught, stayed around after the game, to smooth out the dirt area around the bag, raking the pebbles to guard against another poor bounce the next day.

That's when the gleam in the sand was noticed. And believe it or not, boys and girls, those pebbles he was raking proved to be gold nuggets.

And that first baseman not only was not released, he went on to buy the ballclub with his newfound wealth.

You get the idea. These imaginative concoctions were referred to as "Bill Stern stories." The hero usually turned out to be a popular celebrity. It could be a movie star or a senator or even a president.

One day I bumped into Bill at the studio, and smilingly told him my favorite Bill Stern story involved both of us. That it was a thrill to be introduced by him every week, particularly since he had once suggested I think about pursuing another field.

I reminded him of our previous meeting and added I was having so much fun broadcasting that I hadn't found time to look elsewhere as yet.

We both smiled, and I told him again how much I admired his work.

Our paths crossed many times after that. In fact, when

Bill eventually left NBC, being replaced by Lindsey Nelson, he popped up at ABC where I was paired with him on college games, as his color commentator.

And every time we were together, Bill always apologized, over my protests, about his insensitivity in suggesting I seek another field. I guess Dad's friend had spoken to him and it weighed on his mind.

When I joined Madison Square Garden, Bill used to call or write to me about my work — with words of praise. His luster had begun to fade, but his attentiveness continued.

This charming gentleman with abundant talent and a courtly manner had a problem I was not aware of until our ABC relationship began.

I knew that, as a result of an automobile accident, he had an artificial leg; but I didn't realize that the painkillers he had taken had made him an addict, a problem that was now plaguing him all the way to the broadcast booth.

As I sat side by side with him and heard some of the emotional exaggerations which sometimes entered his work, I began to wonder whether this was an overextended imagination or a perception that was chemically induced.

In particular, there was a Navy-Maryland game in which the Navy quarterback limped off the field before halftime with what appeared to be a knee injury. There were no sideline reporters in those days, so we relied on the team's public relations director to get down to the locker room, determine the extent of the injury, and then relay the word to the radio booth.

Bill anguished over the youngster's injury, and then as the words flowed out and his eyes filled with tears, the seriousness of what might have happened resulted in phrases such as "possibly career-threatening," "might have ended a brilliant future," and "when he left, it's possible the Middies' hope for winning went right with him."

When the next half started and the same quarterback was on the field, Bill became eloquent as he described the amazing medical work by Navy doctors that made it possible for the courageous young man to continue, fighting against pain, and pleading with the medics to let him continue instead of going to the hospital.

It was such a moving narration that I felt as if I were in a movie theater watching two screens at once — the one showing the actual field activity — the other showing what had taken place behind the scenes through a visualization without a camera on hand to record it.

At the Sugar Bowl sometime after this, Bill was not able to go on, and Ray Scott, his color man, stepped into the breach with a top-notch performance of his own.

I liked Bill Stern — and I took pride in his liking me. As a talent on the airwaves — at his best he was unsurpassed in holding listeners glued to their sets with radio calls that embodied the voice art at its very best. And contrary to popular myth, he was extremely accurate in his play calls, at least in those games where I watched him work. He had the right names and numbers.

But Bill's drug problem eventually caught up with him as did his penchant for stretching the truth. He had great talent, though, and hopefully will be remembered for the major contributions he made to early sportscasting — a voice to be remembered.

Ted Husing was a fastidious dresser, epitomizing the deep-throated standouts of bygone radio days. He played the part, emphasizing the richness of his voice, carefully articulating each syllable, and imparting an aura of stardom from his well-selected tie to the scent of cologne that left a distinct impression on every handshake.

In his desire to escape the crassness of reality in a sport as brutal as boxing, Husing once described a bloody nose as "claret coming from his nostrils" incurring the wrath of bleacher bums who wondered "what's dat toikey speakin' about?"

Husing intoned each word to give it a life of its own. His calls boomed out over the airwaves with a distinctive rhythm and cadence — the studied, precise sportscaster, listening to his own words to make sure each one hit the right note. The traditional radio pose was a hand cupped over an ear.

It wasn't until Husing's later years that our paths crossed in a broadcast booth. We both were at Michie Stadium at West Point covering Army football for different networks.

Prior to the game, I had to pass by his booth, and noted a black cloth spread over what appeared to be some sort of electronic machine in front of his microphone. It provoked my curiosity, but I didn't think any more about it until later when I overheard a conversation along press row about Ted's health. The one thing a sportscaster needs most is good eyesight to follow the play, and apparently Ted's sight was the subject of great concern.

Sadly it developed, this great sportscaster was gradually losing this vital function, but he was making a valiant effort to still call games, placing the greatest reliance on his spotter. That was his close friend, Jimmy Dolan, who later became the sports director for CBS.

The carefully guarded machine that had been covered by the black cloth was a spotting board with lights. Jimmy would press a button which would light up the name and number of

the ballcarrier and the tackler. Staying just a scant beat behind the play, Ted could see enough of the field action to know
where the play went, but he couldn't distinguish the numbers
anymore. For that, he relied on his light machine and Dolan's
quickness in pressing the correct button.

Husing's talent was so great he was able to do games in
this fashion, but eventually the sight problem forced him to
give up his sportscasting career. He brought his famed voice
back to the studio where he now turned to music, introducing
records and intoning commercial spots.

Like his competitor Bill Stern, Husing was one of the great
ones.

Harry Wismer got a late start on ABC but made up for that
quickly by bringing an exciting and distinctive voice to the
sports scene, plus a politician's sense of how to win votes — in
this case hiring votes — to attain choice jobs.

It was not uncommon for Harry to bring to a football game
a list of 50 or more key names whom he would plug during the
action — all of whom might be of assistance in attaining some
future assignment. "He's tackled on the 30-yard line," Harry
would exult, "right in front of Sam Jones, the talented advertising executive from Cunningham and Walsh who's here
watching the game today."

This did not always go over too well with the executive's
wife who had last heard that Sam was in the office that day
working on a new campaign. If Harry was trying to be the
broadcaster for the upcoming Army-Navy game, one would
discover that the general and admiral who might influence the
decision along with their ad agency executive and the network
sports director were his guests in the booth, and could antici-

pate their being saluted individually on the air for "the great job they're doing for our country."

Plugs poured out for writers who might help his cause and for organizations that might give him an award.

After a while, this became so obvious that it was tolerated only as buffoonery. Even Harry laughed at this method of doing business, but it did work to catapult him into coveted assignments and into a leading role on the sportscasting scene.

In later years Harry seemed to work harder on soliciting sponsors than on-game preparation.

With less time to concentrate on rules or numbers, Harry began to wing it, occasionally arriving just before airtime and relying on his natural ability to pull him through.

He hadn't done much basketball when, in conjunction with the Sugar Bowl football game, he added its college basketball tournament.

The championship game ended in a tie at the end of regulation time, and that's how he called it — "a tie game."

Listeners were then aware of mumbling off-mike, and finally Harry's excited voice came back with an unusual proclamation.

"Folks, I want to congratulate the Sugar Bowl Committee. They have just ruled there will be a winner of the basketball game, and have decided they will play a five-minute overtime. I think that's an excellent decision, and I want to applaud them for that."

Harry had the talent to become one of the all-time greats if his attention to the commercial side had not overridden the time spent on honing his natural sportscasting abilities. Even so, he conveyed excitement at the microphone and stayed at the top for a long time with many excellent calls.

On the other network — Mutual — a gentleman with a large physique, Hollywood-type looks, well-modulated voice and a calm authority — Al Helfer — was the shining light. I began as his color man, became his back-up play-by-play announcer, and then eventually was assigned to top roles of my own in bowl games, the World Series, and other Mutual sports programs. Al was a delight to work with, always considerate, and I enjoyed his company and that of his wife, Ramona, a gifted popular singer, for many years.

One of the first plaques I ever received was one from Al commemorating my work with him on the 1951 Gator Bowl game. It hangs in my den and still brings back many happy memories of our days together. The word "great" applies to him, also.

Chapter 26

Check-Off List

Talking on the air for any length of time — is never a problem. Getting the opportunity to do so — well, that can be a problem.

I rarely said "no" to an overload. That second chance might not come again. And, as a freelancer, I was paid by the game.

For many years airing the National Invitation Basketball Tournament, I'd call two games in the afternoon and two more at night.

And it was routine in baseball to broadcast all innings of a doubleheader along with all the pre- and post-game shows.

I found it challenging and remunerative to broadcast a college football game on a Saturday afternoon, a pro basketball or ice hockey game that night, and then fly to another city for a pro football telecast the next day. Reminded me of cramming for college exams. Hard work but fun, and it sure beat the alternative.

One hot day in Kansas City, I began a baseball broadcast talk-marathon at one in the afternoon and didn't physically leave the mike until nine o'clock. That was a solo job on a doubleheader, with the shows around it. To top off the day, the second game went to extra innings.

Frankly, I was never concerned about my voice holding up, no matter how spirited the game or how often I'd raise my voice to capture the excitement of a touchdown, a home run, a winning basket, or a hockey goal.

Technique helped a lot. When it comes to explosive moments, I never shout or yell, as a fan in the stands might do. I always sing the high notes, as a vocalist might do on stage. The calls come out clear, without strain or raspiness, and I never felt I was misusing my vocal chords.

Most people talk all day in other lines of work, too. It's not that different, except sportscasting requires more sustained use of the voice, a more animated pitch, and, in moments of excitement, higher notes.

I never worry anymore about my voice than a businessman might. He's on the phone a great part of the day, alternately calm and excited. Voices hold up very well.

With a cup of water and a box of Vicks cough drops in the booth, I'd just start talking.

However, on my check-off list of things to do before every broadcast, there is one item I never overlooked — my last bit of preparation before I settled in behind the mike or in front of the camera for the opening standup.

A vital last step — a visit to the men's room.

So, in addition to a voice that has served me well professionally for over half a century, I know that I also owe a debt of gratitude to my kidneys and bladder. At times they've been sorely tested.

Austin Peay was playing part of a college basketball doubleheader at Madison Square Garden. It is mandatory to check pronunciations personally with the players, before going on air. "Personally" doesn't mean with PR people, coaches, trainers, or fans. It means with the players themselves. It's also vital to check pronunciations of their hometowns, and if need be, their schools. Example: Notre Dame is No-tra Dom, not No-ter Dayme. Of course, popular usage is permitted, although this doesn't mean it's correct.

Too often, a player's name is mispronounced right from the start of his career, and all those around him adopt the incorrect version as the right one. The player doesn't want to embarrass people by correcting them. Only the player knows how he wants his name pronounced, and he's the one who should be asked.

Along those lines, after speaking with the player, I always informed the public address announcer before the game that I had checked on the correct pronunciations and then went over these with him so we'd be in synchronization. Nothing worse than saying one name on the air and having the P.A. man come in loud and clear with a different version.

So it was that I checked with Austin Peay.

Between games while I was conducting interviews, a large contingent of Austin Peay fans arrived for the second game, took their seats in a special rooting section, and let the other Garden folks know they had arrived.

Their chant began just below my mike position, and steadily got louder, an incessant refrain that began to totally consume my thoughts.

"Let's go Pee," "Let's go Pee," "Let's go Pee."

They didn't stop. Their suggestion became a command. A command I couldn't follow.

I had a whole second game to televise — it would take a minimum of three to four minutes to sprint from the TV booth to the nearest men's room — that's a lot of dead air.

"Let's go Pee" — I began to perspire — stood up — maybe that would help. I tried standing on one leg, then the other. It was torture I couldn't share with the viewers. Has a sportscaster ever said, "Pardon me folks, I have to go to the men's room." Finally, we went to commercial. Mercifully I was saved when broadcast analyst Cal Ramsey returned to the booth. "Cal," I whispered, "take over, give the lineups, the cues, intro the anthem — I've got to make a quick pit stop." I scrambled out of the booth, raced to the men's room, and made it back just before the opening tip.

Yes, I had the pronunciation right, but, I'll tell you, it would have been a lot easier night if the chant had been, "Let's go Pay."

Chapter 27

The Show Goes On

You don't see it on camera, but sportscasters do cough, sneeze, clear their throats, go to the bathroon, eat meals, pay bills, attend parent-teacher meetings, and, in essence, are no different than anyone else.

Except that, unlike stage shows, there's no understudy standing by if a problem arises. If the sportscaster commits to broadcasting a game, a schedule, or a full season, he's expected to do it and do it well, regardless of what else is happening in his life.

That includes normal illness. Somehow, in over 50 years of broadcasting, I've never missed a play-by-play assignment. Along the way I surmounted high temperatures, sore throats, stuffed noses, and any other ailment which might have kept me in bed. My job was to be there, prepared and ready.

As a freelancer for most of those years, paid for each game I broadcast, I knew that the show had to go on for four reasons. I wanted to get paid. I enjoyed the work. If I were out of the lineup, there was always the chance that my temporary re-placement might become a permanent one. And the personal vanity to always fulfill an assignment.

To keep my streak going, doctors' and dentists' appointments had to be sandwiched in at odd hours.

In Washington, one baseball season, I bit down too hard on a frozen ice cream bar and broke a tooth. That happened after a night game, and I had a day game to follow. Immediate action was vital.

Dr. Michael Oliveri, my dentist, let me in his office at 2 A.M. and did the repair work in his pajamas. I was back on the air that afternoon.

One off-season I came down with the chicken pox, but still had a nightly radio show to do. I broadcast from my bed with the engineer outside the bedroom door for his protection.

The show goes on — and the audience expects a cheerful upbeat sportscaster, regardless of how he may feel. They don't want to hear any complaints that the sportscaster is tired or too hot, or ill, or upset. The sportscaster is paid to perform every day.

I remember my first encounter with root canal surgery. I really had no idea what that meant or what it entailed. I was living in Westchester County, New York, at the time and was referred to a dentist with an outstanding reputation — Dr. Marvin Firdman. Could I go right back on the air that night? That was my primary consideration.

I arrived in the morning at his White Plains, New York, office, apprehensive about the procedure, and how long the recuperation period would take.

I sat in the waiting room, skimmed through a magazine, and was finally called. Dr. Firdman was busy studying an X-ray. He waved to me to sit in his dentist chair, put down the X-ray, and then I saw the needle.

"Open please."

"Is this novocaine?"

"Yes, it is."

"Is this necessary?"

"I would recommend it."

"Doctor, before you start, please let me speak to you. I don't know what you have to do. Would you please give me a play-by-play as you go along so that I know what's going on. If it's going to be painful, just tell me about how long it will last and I'll prepare myself to take it. I'm assuming I'll be okay to do my broadcast tonight. Am I right? When will the novocaine wear off? Will there be any swelling? I've got to be on TV tonight."

The doctor gripped the needle in his beefy paws, stared at me with disdain, and then bellowing like a staff sergeant, cowed me with his belligerent response.

"I'm a dentist — not a play-by-play man. I don't do conversations. I work without questions and answers. You'll be able to broadcast tonight.

"When I say 'open your mouth,' open it. When I say 'close,' close it. Occasionally I may say 'spit out.' If so, spit.

"Now those are the rules. No exceptions. No questions. Is that understood? If so, I'll begin."

I said nothing. He gave me the novocaine injection.

I was too shocked to utter a word. He saw me looking at his hands, now wrapped around a drill. And then as he began, he added these words. "I don't know why I ever entered this root canal field in the first place. I've got the wrong hands for this job. Much too large."

He saw the look of fear come into my eyes, and sensed that he had won the battle for my silence.

"Open a little wider please," he said, and I meekly complied.

There was no play-by-play until I returned to the mike later that night. And I must admit, Dr. Firdman, without my questions, did a very good job.

I've been fortunate. I've been blessed with a resilient body, and a team of talented and understanding doctors and dentists who, when needed, helped me get ready for broadcast action. I'm most grateful to them.

It helps also that I live with a nurse — my wife.

Chapter 28

Hockey Secrets

Many ballplayers don't think ahead to the moves they're about to make to help them win.

Well, that may be a little strong, so let me start again.

Most players, particularly the great ones, react to the situation. The thinking has already been pre-processed into reflex actions. No time to think and react. It has to be instantaneous.

That's why so few superstars become good coaches or managers. In addition to the frustration of coping with others who can't play up to the stars' standards, trying to teach what they never had to learn in the first place is too difficult a task.

There are some great players, though, who are Hall-of-Famers through a combination of both physical and mental attributes. Andy Bathgate, a former New York Ranger great, not only played his way to the top, he also planned his way there.

The key word with Andy was "perceptive."

A good-looking, personable guy, Andy enjoyed the interplay with fans and earned an immediate spot in their hearts. Andy was a natural as the Rangers' captain and the leader of the team.

"Bob," Andy questioned me one day, "are you a natural righthander, or a lefty?"

"I'm right-handed, Andy, why do you ask?"

"Because I've noticed that, as we walked through the Garden together, twice as we came to a door, you took two little steps before you approached the door and then used your left hand to open it. Just struck me as unusual."

I would never notice this, nor care, but that was Andy. He saw what others never noticed, with an amazing ability to counteract in advance what opponents would do. He was prepared to top them before he took the ice.

As a teenager, I had been to four or five hockey games at Madison Square Garden and was impressed with the speed and spectacle of the sport, but my inside knowledge consisted of knowing that to score you had to put the puck into the net, or at least across the line the goalie was guarding. The red light would then flash on and the crowd would go wild. Was there something more I needed to know to enjoy the game?

My closest association to the sport was on rollerskates. There was a parking garage behind our home, and, on the cracked cement, with litter in the crevices and a few broken bottles as playing hazards, we'd take some splintered sticks, place a couple of cans apart at either end signifying the goal area, and have some spirited two-on-two competitions while coping with skinned knees, bruises, occasional cuts, and whacks against our unprotected bodies. We never gave much thought to safety; after all, we were just playing a game.

Many years later, when TV was first born in Washington, DC, I telecast all the sports events on WTTG, including a minor league team called the Washington Hockey Lions. I added some knowledge about blue lines, red lines, and "icing the puck" to my repertoire and was ready to go. I also learned hockey players are a rare breed. Those Lions didn't hesitate to go to the

152

medical room when they were cut. They had insurance policies calling for $10 a stitch. For some, that was their only chance for a steak that week. "Just one more stitch, Doc, okay?"

I soon landed at Madison Square Garden televising all its events, including the New York Rangers. To be authoritative on the broadcasts, it was mandatory I learn the finesses of the game, techniques, strategies, rules, moves — all the inside details that a well-informed sportscaster should impart to the viewers along with the play-by-play.

I gained knowledge through asking questions. Being curious is a great asset, probing until every mystery is cleared, until I knew the answers. Reading will add to learning, of course, but the give and take of questioning can have a great impact in obtaining immediate knowledge.

There was no doubt as to whom I'd approach first. I had admired Bathgate's play, liked his outward-going manner, his friendliness, and the pleasure he received from discussing his sport.

So I enlisted Andy's support, bought a notebook, labeled it "Bathgate Notes," and on road trips sat beside him on planes, ate with him after the games, and learned what inside hockey was really all about, while filling page after page with his views and comments. We became close friends, and quite aside from note-taking, enjoyed each other's company.

The time came when there were no more basic questions to ask. Andy had given me all his answers. They were now filed in notebooks and implanted in my mind. More important, learning the fine points had increased my appreciation of the sport and enhanced my call of the games.

One night, having dinner after a game, I said, "Andy, all those hockey notes you gave me — are those answers to my questions the same answers I'd get from other pro players or are your views different?"

"I think you'll find, Bob, that my methods and techniques are strictly my own. Others may have come to the same conclusions but I've never been a copier. The stuff I've told you works for me, and it's what I recommend for others, but I guess you might call them my secrets."

And that's when the idea took hold. "Andy, I've got a great idea. Why don't I put our notes together in book form, and find a publisher? *Andy Bathgate's Hockey Secrets* will be the title. I'll write it from our notes and conversations. This will give a lot of kids in the U.S. and Canada a chance to learn from your tips and methods. What do you say?"

Andy thought it was a great idea as did the Prentice-Hall Publishing Company when I brought them the manuscript. I enlisted Associated Press hockey writer Hal Bock to give it a further lookover, and soon it was ready for the bookstores.

In those comparatively early days of hockey with just a few how-to-play books on the market, the book zoomed to number one on the sports sales list. Ironically, I found myself in great demand, as co-author, as an authority on inside hockey. There were TV and radio appearances, newspaper columns, the praise mounted, and, in Canada, where hockey was king, the book was hailed by the media.

Sales were booming, another edition of the book came out in Swedish, and I could sense no letdown in sight.

Until Andy was traded to Toronto. Nothing wrong with that of course. It might give us another boost in Canadian sales — except for one problem. The cover was a full-length picture of Andy in a Rangers' uniform, not exactly a good sales enticement for Maple Leaf fans.

Prentice-Hall, wanting to keep sales alive, made a great concession. They changed the cover on all remaining books to show Andy in a Toronto uniform. And the book moved into new printings. Until Andy was traded to Detroit.

By this time, other players had jumped into the book market, and we decided that one cover change was enough.

We eventually lost bestseller class, but sales continued.

I did learn three lessons from this venture, though:

1. If one uses a cover shot of a star, put him in street clothes, not a team uniform.

2. Becoming an "expert" can be accomplished with a great deal of curiosity, and a good friend who answers questions.

3. Success comes from content that's well received by readers and critics. From an inner reward standpoint, that's the goal.

Chapter 29

Wise Guys

Can brainpower win championships?

Absolutely, if the team also has great talent, excellent coaching, and perhaps the most important extra ingredient — unselfishness. An unselfish team enjoys assisting each other toward the common goal and making that more important than individual glory.

The smartest team that I ever covered as a play-by-play telecaster was the 1969-1970 New York Knicks as they won their first championship.

For years, basketball coaches have stressed fundamentals, explaining over and over that execution is the foundation for success. That Knick team proved that proper performance of the basics not only was the way to win but was also thrilling to watch.

Their coach, Red Holzman, stressed defense, and the chant "Dee-fense" reverberated through Madison Square Garden. It was a treat for the fans to watch a concept become a reality. Defense meant hard work, sacrifice, eyeing the ball, boxing out, rebounding, playing the defensive angle, switching quickly when necessary, establishing defensive position, maximum effort under the boards, quick hands, pressing when needed, diving for loose balls, guarding your opponent with tenacity — all in all, giving a complete effort to the unglamorous but vital part of the game.

On offense, unselfishness included self-discipline in shot selection. Hitting the open man received the most applause from the savvy Knick fans. Sinking the shot was the end result.

That Knick team was not broken down into specialists — or specialist terms. No labels were needed. No one specified the "point guard" or "shooting guard." Forwards were not classified as "small" or "power." A center was expected to pass, shoot, rebound, block shots, and jam. Each man was expected to play his position in every way. Those Knicks had something else in common — great hands. They whipped the ball from one to the other. It just hummed — in and out — side to side — in the corner, back out — finally the free man — for the best shot. And those same hands on defense made steals an important part of the offensive attack. The defense helped make the offense.

The reserves accepted their roles and were proud of their contributions. Team came first — minutes played — who started or who finished — were unimportant when weighed against the final score. There was no groaning, no public cries for more time, no contract renegotiation, no demand for trades, no hiding in the trainer's room, no surliness, no conflict with the coach, no agent interference — just basketball as a team sport — and basketball at its finest.

There was a very telling and unusual statistic at season's end. No member of this unselfish championship team was in the top 10 in league scoring. They earned their A's in assists.

There was also a professionalism to this group that made them stand out in another and most important way. They were just as approachable and unflappable in defeat as they were in victory.

They didn't exult in winning. They didn't moan or cry or hang their heads in losing. They accepted the "ups and downs" of sport and the atmosphere of the locker room didn't change. They were professionals, admired as individuals and as a team.

That professionalism emanated from their coach Red Holzman and his trainer and goodwill man Danny Whelan, aided by their lively PR man Frankie Blauschild. When the game was over, it was over. They could smile, win or lose. Losses hurt, of course, they always do, and a substandard performance is a blow to pride, but this was not revealed in post-game behavior. It was professionalism at its finest.

I used to marvel at Red's post-game press conferences. Along with his modest, self-effacing comments about victories, or calm, unperturbed "that's life" remarks about a loss, were disclosures about where he might dine that night, or remarks about an old movie he had seen the night before — all interspersed with positive comments about his team. Red did not dwell on winning at the buzzer or an occasional off-night on the court. His team responded in the same composed manner. No peaks of exhilaration or periods of remorse. That was yesterday's story. Red always reminded his questioners, "there'll be a new day tomorrow."

It was remarkable to view their mental discipline after watching so many teams and individuals who, unfortunately, never learned how to adjust to the turbulence of their profession. Most top pros learn how to win, but not all know how to cope with losing. To remain gracious in defeat is no easy matter.

The players showed wisdom in knowing how to deal with

others. They also had great intelligence, recognized on and off the court with achievements.

Just check out this starting lineup:

Coach:
- Red Holzman — Coach and General Manager. Hall of Fame.

Forwards:
- Bill Bradley — Rhodes Scholar and New Jersey Senator. Hall of Fame.
- Dave DeBusschere — Coach, Commissioner, and General Manager. Hall of Fame.

Guards:
- Walt Frazier — Radio and TV personality, and renowned wordsmith. Hall of Fame.
- Dr. Dick Barnett — Masters and Doctorate. Number retired at Madison Square Garden.

Center:
- Willis Reed — Coach and General Manager. Hall of Fame.

And these brainy reserves: Phil Jackson (Coach, Chicago Bulls), Cazzie Russell, Dave Stallworth, Mike Riordan, John Warren, Bill Hosket, Nate Bowman, and Don May.

Trainer:
- Danny Whelan — Doctorate of good humor.

The applauding crowd was also smart. They gobbled up 13 books about this team, and, as if on cue in unison, chants filled the Garden, making each game an event. The spectators seemed to have total rapport with the players, imparting a special glow to a unifying experience.

I had the good fortune to be behind the TV mike also for the '73 crown, where new members of the cast included memory expert Jerry Lucas with his long-range bombs, and the Magic man, Earl "The Pearl" Monroe, whose extraordinary moves brought "oohs" and "ahs" of appreciation. Like their championship predecessors, they, too, had no Knicks in the league's top 10 scorers, but won as a well-rounded team.

That teamwork extended to the Madison Square Garden TV booth where a close bond of friendship with Cal Ramsey and myself and our unerring stat man Harry Robinson made calling games together a delight.

Red had an ability to combine discipline with compassion —and a bit of humor. He carried with him a large conductor's watch in an old-fashioned fob pocket of his pants. As round as a miniature pizza, Red told me the watch cost him $2.00 many years ago. It's a true heirloom.

But Red relied on that watch. And when Earl Monroe was late for a plane takeoff, Red greeted him with watch in hand, and the penalty already in place. "That will cost you $100, Earl, because that's our rule. Lucky you're just late — or you'd have to buy a plane ticket, too. Now Earl," and a twinkle came to Red's eyes, "I know you may be thinking this old watch doesn't keep accurate time and you shouldn't be fined. I agree — it's a pretty old watch, and maybe it's off a minute or so. But you're having a great year, Earl, so you might consider, at Christmas time, buying me a new watch, and then we can both be sure this won't happen again." Earl laughed, Red smiled, and the point was made. And when Red's accomplice, trainer Danny Whelan added his good-natured needling, re-spect off-the-court helped to produce victories on it.

Phil Rizzuto, admired as a Yankee shortstop and loved as a broadcaster, on my Senators' post-game show.

With quotable Yogi Berra. Yogi's advice about a restaurant:
"Nobody goes there anymore—it's too crowded."

With "The Babe."

When it's talking about hitting, Ted Williams is a man for all ages.

Vice President Richard Nixon and daughter Tricia. On a between-games radio show, I selected "at random" a "man in the stands" to interview. At program's end, the "government worker" revealed his name.

Casey Stengel always drew a crowd. One question would trigger enough material for an entire program—some of which I even understood.

Power hitter Larry Doby pioneered the entry of African-American players into the American League.

In every way, Whitey Ford was in total control when he was on the mound.

*"Saying hey"
to Willie Mays.*

One of my favorite managers and strategists, Al Lopez.

Beginning as a teenager, Maury Povich, on my left, soon became my right-hand man, too. He was my statistician at this time, helped in my show productions, and later took a turn at the mike. Maury remains the closest of friends. On my right here is broadcaster Jack Guinan.

The time difference encountered in Australia while telecasting the Surfing Carnival was anything but an eye-opener for me. "You should have seen the surf yesterday," they told us on arrival, as we viewed the calm waters.

The same year I interviewed Brooke Shields at the National Horse Show, I had a less-publicized highlight. I made equine history by leading a horse to water—and proving he would drink—right out of my water bucket. I captured that major feat on tape, but Brooke was the center of attention.

Bill Dana was a hit with comedy, Mickey Mantle was a hit on either side of the plate, and I—well, I just talked.

Play-by-play telecasting on NBC-TV Baseball "Game-of-the-Week."

A proud moment when I joined forces with Joe Garagiola on NBC-TV. A talented partner, a fine man.

At the Millrose Games with Robin Campbell on my right and Don Paige on my left. A live telecast of the Games was always a challenging experience with quick switches from one event to the next.

In 33 years doing the bark-by-bark at the Westminster Kennel Club Dog Show, no dog ever uttered an unkind word about me.

A look behind the scenes at the "Game-of-the-Week."

With noted track star Carl Lewis.

*July 30, 1995. Induction Day into the Broadcasters' Wing of the Baseball
Hall of Fame. Hall-of-Famer Ralph Kiner presented me with the Ford
Frick Award.*

All those years have wonderful rewards.

Chapter 30

A Walk through the Garden

My first thoughts were of the Astrodome. You may remember when the gigantic structure was erected in Houston. Its main occupant would be the Houston Astros baseball team.

Soon after this new domed indoor stadium was first unveiled, the baseball team worked out and praise was lavish — except for one flaw.

Fielders could not find a ball hit up in the air.

A rather embarrassing problem.

Seems the white ball didn't show up against the sunlight pouring in from a battery of windowpanes in the roof. By the time the fielders got a sighting, the ball would descend far out of reach.

After colored baseballs proved ineffective, with some ingenuity the problem was resolved. The glass panes were painted, eliminating the outside light. Fielders could now see the ball.

But with no sunlight coming in, the grass withered and died.

And so friends, artificial Astroturf came into being. A green carpet was installed. The sharp, higher bounce of the ball brought about new offensive and defensive strategies.

We switch now to the spanking new Madison Square Garden, which opened above Pennsylvania Station in 1968.

Unlike the previous Garden with its cliff-like heights where one looked directly down on the players, the new Garden ascended gradually. Sightline planning may not have considered the need to look over the near sideboards in hockey or over spectators standing during exciting moments. That situation was eventually aided by installing overhead video.

The Garden also replaced large ornamental railings with thin ones, and the faithful fans, now paying a higher price than at the old Garden, seemed pleased, particularly when the Garden eventually added a superlative light show in introducing the players.

Eventually, the new lush surroundings got another facelift, and the Garden continues as the most magnificent indoor arena in the world. But, as in Houston, an important early adjustment had to be made.

Everything had been readied for Opening Night — a Bob Hope-Bing Crosby extravaganza — with one astounding drawback. There was no press box — for TV, radio, or press.

Oversight or design?

As part of the Madison Square Garden inner circle at the time, I sat in on my first management meeting and was the center of many icy stares when I asked my first question.

"How about the press facilities?"

The silence warned me immediately that I had hit a nerve. Apparently this had been a hot topic long before I made an appearance, and I had an instinctive feeling that discussion and resolution must have been heated.

"Well," finally came one hesitant reply, "we've worked out a system where everyone will be happy."

I realized the caution light was on. Does this put-me-off reply indicate that I'm moving into dangerous territory, or does my reportorial instinct — curiosity — compel me to continue. I decided to take a middle course.

"I'm sure it's all been worked out. I was just curious where the TV booths are located, and the press box, but I'm sure it's somewhere on the diagram. Don't mean to interrupt. I'll check it out later."

"There is no TV booth — no press box."

I had the feeling I was about to descend into a twilight zone. The answer made no sense whatsoever. Should I give with the punch — or spar a bit longer?

"Well, I'm sure there must be a good reason for that — one that I'm just not aware of. I'm curious though — if the question arises — and I'm sure it will — where does the press sit — and where is the TV and radio location? How would I answer?"

I couldn't sense whether the feeling around me was hostility or relief that this issue was now in the open.

"Well, here's the plan. It's based on our calculations that, in addition to basketball and hockey, the Garden is also used for the circus, and ice shows, horse shows, a dog show, rock shows, concerts, conventions, and all the rest. So it would be foolish to make a permanent place for TV, radio, and the press when they don't attend all those other events. That would cut down on our seats and revenue. Those spots could be occupied by paying customers.

"So we worked out a solution. On the nights there's

basketball or hockey, we reserve tickets for the press, and on other nights customers sit in those seats."

I decided to pursue — in a discreet fashion — where the locations would be.

"Well, I understand the concept, but this raises some questions. Let's take the press now. Where do writers do their typing as they file their stories?"

"They'll sit in regular seats in the first level up, and we'll put planks in front of them so they can rest their notepads and typewriters. Those planks will extend across each row."

"What happens if a writer sitting in the middle of any row wants to get up and go to the men's room? How does he get by all those in that row locked in by the same long plank?" I was now warming to the task at hand.

"Well, those are wrinkles we have to work out."

"On the TV side, the broadcaster has to be near his color commentator, statistician, floor director, and engineer. They need monitors in front of them to watch the TV screen. Sitting in seats may make that difficult. Another problem is that the visiting broadcaster should be separated so that his call isn't a distraction. I'm not sure seating in the same open row area will accomplish this. When the broadcasters go on camera, where will the camera be? If you put them near their seats, they'll block people. Camera operators will be standing too. Will there be room for that? Is there a provision for camera placement? How about TV and radio guests and players? Will they have to come up to the seats? Shouldn't there be an interview room? There may be many problems ahead, including a lot of howling from the press, the TV people, the radio guys, and the photographers. Could be very embarrassing."

I refrained from asking from where the suggestion had

come —building the Garden without press facilities — but I knew that at least one person in the management group now viewed me as an adversary, plus all those who had sanctioned these arrangements.

One of the favorite corporate ploys when dealing with potentially embarrassing topics is to refer such matters to committees for further study. Sometimes this results in actions, oftentimes it's just to avoid further debate. In this case, I was asked to look into the entire media matter and suggest some amicable solutions without a loss in revenue.

I worked behind the scenes to minimize the problems and avert a fiery reaction. The first break the Garden had was when the basketball writers, hearing that they might not be courtside, came to management with a unified protest demanding they had to be placed there to cover the games. That request was granted after heated internal haggling that this would interfere with court seats for big-money spenders. The writers won out, and some broadcasters were later placed there too. That left hockey to deal with.

John Halligan, the Rangers' PR director, and I went scouting throughout the building and found a walkway on either side of the arena just at the top of the green seats and below the blues, that was wide enough for chairs, and a writing or broadcasting small table top. We made this the hockey press box, and found additional spaces in overhanging booths at both ends of the ice.

Next were camera positions. We received city permission to lower the top of exitways if we still complied with safety standards. We placed the cameras and operators on top of those exitways, low enough so that they wouldn't interfere with the fans behind them. Eventually a new small broadcast location was constructed on each side of the arena to seat four people and sunk low enough to not block those sitting behind it.

For basketball, TV standups before the game and at halftime were put on the floor, or, in the case of hockey, in a designated TV room close by the dressing rooms — a room with a proper backdrop which could also be used for basketball opens, halftimes, or post-games on camera.

Photographers were given court placements for basketball, and rinkside enclosures for hockey. Hockey writers were informed that their early seats among the paying customers were only temporary and that they soon would be moved to their own location.

Amazingly, a media explosion was averted. Few were aware of the original plan and of the choice seats they almost had to take where, unfortunately, they would not have been able to do their job. Averted was a further inquisition of who had formulated the initial blueprint scheme, and how it had come so close to reality.

Behind the scenes, it was gratifying to have a hand in the scrapping of the original seating plan. Eventually, the situation was aided also by hanging a TV booth from the ceiling, a forerunner of the later luxury boxes. In those pioneer days, one had to ascend a ladder to get into that booth. With subsequent Garden improvements, the ladder has been replaced by steps, and a later addition of a restroom was a great relief in every way.

❖ ❖ ❖

One final note. The original Garden diagrams labeled the exitways as "vomitories." One had to walk through the vomitories to get to the refreshment stands, not a very inviting thought, in either direction. I made my plea that the thought was nauseating, and was finally satisfied when the exitways regained their original name.

Chapter 31

The Showman

Today, they call it sports marketing.

I'm not sure what Chicago White Sox top executive Bill Veeck called it many years ago, but his philosophy was that giving an unexpected bonus today can bring in bigger revenues tomorrow.

This demands some creative thinking, and an understanding of psychology in sales.

I was broadcasting at old Comiskey Park in Chicago the day that Veeck provided an unexpected and unadvertised treat for fans between games of a Sox doubleheader.

At the conclusion of game one, it was time to strike up the band — not just one band, but four of the finest Dixieland bands in the nation, including Louis Armstrong.

Each group, separated from the next, entered in a well-decorated truck, blaring away close to the stands, slowly circling the field. It began in the left-field corner. The first group was followed by a second, and then, in turn, by the third and the fourth.

The loud speaker on each vehicle carried the foot-tapping music right to the fans, a four-star show, the between-games program of the year — at White Sox expense — completely unannounced or publicized in advance. A hit parade of bands.

Later that day, I asked Veeck why he had decided to pick up the tab on this.

"Bob, if I advertised or promoted the bands, days or weeks in advance, it would have helped sales today. No question about that, but I was thinking long-range.

"Every one of our fans today just loved it. For their regular ticket price, they got something extra — for nothing. A gift for showing up.

"So just consider. Each of those fans will go home, tell his family, his neighbors, his friends, his associates, about what the White Sox did yesterday and all for free. It will be a topic of conversation.

"We've got a great chance of bringing them back. Not only today's fans — but all those who were told or read about it or heard about it who want to be on hand for our next unadvertised bonus. They now know the chance exists. And they'll keep showing up more than once, just like playing the lottery.

"Word of mouth is great advertising. And after a few weeks, we'll pull off another stunt, and the process will begin again."

"Great idea, Bill. How come others don't do this?"

"Giving something away for nothing is a little too radical for most of my colleagues. They're thinking day by day, not future."

"I know I'll be talking about it. Were there any other benefits?"

"Just one personal one, Bob, that has nothing to do with sales. I love Dixieland jazz."

Chapter 32

The Wave

I never encountered a sport I didn't enjoy broadcasting, including dog shows and horse shows.

As noted earlier, though, I passed up wrestling — pro variety. Granted these guys are versatile athletes, take a terrific pounding in the ring, are excellent actors, and can win critical acclaim as "heroes" or "villains." Their matches are called "exhibitions," and, like magicians, they're entertaining illusionists. My conscience would not permit me to express honest emotion when calling ballgames, and theatrical emotion describing grunt-and-groaners. Unfortunately, in sports as in TV, movies, and print, violence, contrived or otherwise, is used to attract viewers, readers, and ticket-buyers.

I broadcast many sports that I've played, others I've watched for many years, and others I worked at learning in exactly the same fashion that one studies a new subject in school. Source material includes books, tapes, films, interviews, practice sessions, incessant questioning and note-taking. The trick is getting the assignment. Once I had that in hand, studying is intense — day and night — or spread over weeks — depending on the broadcast date. My notes on each sport are kept in files or boxes, to be added to year after year.

I used the same studying techniques I utilized at Duke University. Countless hours of preparation.

Roone Arledge is the head of ABC News and an innovator in sports production and presentations. Some years ago when I was serving as ABC-TV host for college and pro scoreboard shows, I was walking in the hall outside his office when I bumped into Roone coming out of the elevator.

After exchanging the usual "hiya doings" he added a line that sounded enticing. "Bob, are you busy this coming weekend?"

I thought that maybe an invitation might be forthcoming — maybe a touch football game in Connecticut, perhaps a tennis match, or maybe an added sports show. I contemplated my plans quickly, and decided they could be put on hold for whatever Roone had in mind.

"I'm available if you need me, Roone," I said.

"Do you know anything about surfing?"

I gulped at this one. The real answer was no, but my response was, "Well, I can brush up on a few things and I'll be ready."

"That's great, Bob. We'll get you a ticket and you can be on your way tomorrow."

"Tomorrow, Roone?"

"Yes, tomorrow."

"That's good. To where, Roone?"

"Oh yes, guess I didn't tell you. Australia."

"Did you say Australia, Roone?"

"That's right. You'll like Australia."

"To do what, Roone?"

Roone was smiling. With some others, this might be a put-on, but with Roone, assigning a quick weekend jaunt to Australia could be just a few lines of conversation.

171

"A big event — Wide World of Sports — the Australian Surfing Carnival."

"Sounds exciting, Roone. Do you have any literature on this? Any contacts to discuss this with? Where in Australia, by the way?

"Sydney — a beautiful city. And wait till you see the height of those waves. Tremendous. Chuck Howard is the producer. Just check with him. I've got to go. Have a guy waiting for me in the office."

Australia? Surfing Carnival? I knew I had to work fast to cram in some knowledge. I had to be an authority by the weekend.

Chuck had a few pieces of promotional literature on the event. It seemed that lifeguards from various beaches would be competing in a series of trials — different exercises — to determine which beach team would win the title.

As to what events, what the rules were, who the participants were, or what techniques made for winners, I didn't have a clue. Would ABC-TV pay for a call to Australia to fill me in? Whom would I call? What time is it there?

Never having surfed, I had no personal stories to fall back on. Roone had hit me with one sport I knew just one thing about — that it was done on boards, riding them towards the shore on waves, usually by suntanned Californians.

I was on the plane the next day for my trip halfway around the world.

Day ran into night and night into day.

The next day — or was it the same day or the previous day — with the changing time zones — I was groggy. Jet lag is for real. The body has to be reconditioned to new eating and sleeping times — and quickly.

I met my Australian analyst, we looked at the selected TV

beach, and I noted that life in Sydney, Australia, appeared to be an outgrowth of what was happening in the United States. Same movies, same TV shows on tape, same performers in night clubs. The biggest difference was driving on the opposite side of the street and hearing English accents.

I found it difficult to shake the cobwebs. I woke up at three in the morning with my body clock on New York time and was so sleepy at dinner I dozed off while writing broadcast notes. Meanwhile, I learned that I would be covering everything from a marathon swim to the big surfing finals. In between, there'd be a timed competition on the launching of a rescue boat, beach events, and a parade of lifeguards.

The day of the telecast arrived and I was barely coming out of my trance. I was awake enough, however, to notice that the big waves for surfing had disappeared. There just weren't any high enough to muster any excitement. Barely more than ripples. It would take some creative camera angles to make this look any more imposing than splashing around in a bathtub.

"That's a shame," said our Australian host. "Too bad you weren't here last week. You can't believe how high they were then." Lines that had a familiar ring.

The telecast went well with the beach events, but I knew I was in deep water when they started the long-distance swimming race. Contestants were to go around a distant buoy, and back.

Heads were bobbing in the water miles away — just heads — no number on a forehead for identification — no strategy — just arms in and out of the water — swimming farther and farther away. My job? To keep talking intelligently, creatively. To hold audience.

I wasn't hired to just keep saying, "they're still swimming, folks," so I called on another avenue of opportunity —

imagination — peppering my Australian analyst with my "what if" inquiries.

"A little faltering, it appears, by the lead swimmer, wearing the blues of the Apollo Club. There's the possibility of a fatigue problem, and occasionally there's the unexpected peril of cramps — always a danger in longer races. What precautions do the lifeguards take against these possibilities?"

Or.

"There's always an ever-present fear — rarely discussed — but one can't eliminate the possibility — sharks." This question opened up a gruesome field of exploration, in fact more than I had anticipated. The analyst added credibility to my inquiry by remarking there was a bell that would ring if sharks were ever sighted. I spoke further about what a terrifying sound that must be. The element of danger now became a dramatic part of an uneventful race.

And so it went — for miles — as I badgered my Australian counterpart for his opinion on all the perils, maladies, and attacks that could thwart these swimmers, along with my running account of the honor that was at stake in winning these lifeguard battles, and some upbeat views on their real mission — protecting the safety of those who might venture too far from shore.

Before the day was over, we explored the diet of these marathon contestants, discussed whether they were considered amateurs or pros, whether there should be future Olympic competition, how each beach vied to get the superior lifeguards, why women were not in competition. I ran the gamut — as heads kept bobbing — until one finally came across the finish line. My shouts of exultation at watching a winner emerge were made in relief — mine.

Chapter 33

Inaugurals

The TV pioneer medium was gaining momentum. Radio columnists were finally beginning to take a peek at the magic box with the flickering black and white images and the exorbitant price tag. It was still being sold as a large piece of furniture with beautiful paneling around a small set. Sports, studio shows, and a few old western movies comprised the bill of fare. And I was going as far coast-to-coast as national coverage would extend.

It was a historic event. Television was going to be seen as far west as St. Louis. Nineteen-forty-nine was the year, and I was selected by the DuMont Network to be its announcer on a pooled telecast for the Presidential Inaugural. The major networks would supply their radio luminaries. NBC had Ben Grauer and CBS had Doug Edwards.

Why was a sportscaster chosen? The decision was based on ad-libbing ability. That's what I did every day on ballgames, so why not on news? There were no organized TV news departments in those days as there are today. In fact, news was not considered a salable product.

Having started my TV career in 1946 as Washington's first

telecaster, I understood that the words had to accompany the video. Pictures and sound had to synchronize. That knowledge helped me prepare. The Presidential Inaugural would consist of floats and bands coming down Pennsylvania Avenue, making a turn, and then passing by the President's reviewing stand in front of the White House.

That meant that, except for a few interviews with spectators, the camera would be focused on the floats. But what was on the floats? I figured knowing that would be key to my commentary.

I was the only video visitor to the National Airport where the floats were being put together in hangars. Each float had a specific theme, usually with exhibitions extolling the products of the state or its historic accomplishments, or old buildings or landmarks, or distinguished citizens or modern achievements — and I wrote down exactly what each depiction would be. When the camera zoomed in, I knew specifically what was being represented.

My early training in TV proved valuable in the success of that telecast. At the other camera locations, my distinguished colleagues, brought up in radio, read extensive notes about past inaugurals and presidential history. But increasingly, the producer and director returned to me to explain what was being seen on TV screens. Eventually, they just stayed with me to finish out the day. My belief in how to prepare for TV had proved correct — the words have to mesh with the pictures — a new concept at that time.

In 1953, the Mutual Broadcasting System asked me to be its anchor man on the inaugural, sitting across from President Eisenhower at his reviewing stand. That became a newsworthy position when a cowboy, twirling a lasso in the parade, let fly at the standing President, and roped him with arms pinned at his side, just like a steer in a Wild West competition. FBI agents scurried to the President's side, untangling the momentarily helpless Chief Executive while the bands played on. That proved to be the story of the day, with its alarming possibilities.

Since those early days, TV news departments have been formed and have hired newsmen who can ad-lib. They have also learned that advance research necessitates dealing with any visual aspect which demands explanation.

I'd love to watch a tape of that first Presidential Inaugural telecast, but there was no tape in those early days. I'm curious if I really started the show by saying, "Hi sports fans," as one viewer says he thought he'd heard. Frankly, had I done so, my close friend Bill Gold, who was by my side at both inaugurals, would have whispered a correction in my ear. Bill, an outstanding *Washington Post* columnist and *Washington Post* radio station news director, worked with me diligently on preparation, and at the site. He compiled photos of Washington politicians who might be in the presidential party to make sure I could identify them quickly by sight, with proper title, and, if need be, proper state. No one ever calls to say you're right, but just make a mistake, and the phones start ringing and the mail piles up.

Nothing like being prepared, and, come to think of it, there's not much difference between calling a football game and an inaugural. Identification is what counts.

Chapter 34

Going to the Dogs

Eddie Layton, organist for the Yankees, and in past years for the Knicks, Rangers, and Islanders, came up with a can't-miss idea. It was based upon my Westminster Kennel Club Dog Show songs, one of which I'd weave in every year along with my bark-by-bark canine commentary.

I provided the vocalizing and the lyrics, Eddie the musical accompaniment, and what had started out as a stunt eventually became a tradition.

Typical words from a closing number:

"And now it's goodbye

"Let's watch the credits roll

"Westminster Show

"For dogs, the Super Bowl...."

I'm not sure how humans responded to the yearly songfest, although the mail and calls were positive, but I do know this — no dog ever had an unkind word for me.

Eddie's big plan: "Bob, we've been taping your dog show songs for many years so here's my idea. Why don't we put them all together in a dog show album? Could be a hit record. We'll put a George Kalinsky picture on the cover and we can't miss."

I pondered Eddie's suggestion. It was an exciting thought

— maybe a dog food manufacturer would invest — but I had to pose the question: "Eddie, it would be fun to do a dog show album, but how many dogs will buy it?"

That project is still on hold.

The Westminster Show was serious business, but in between group judging, there was time for a lighthearted approach. One year I gathered a large group of champion dogs in the Knicks' locker room, put on my jersey with the word "Coach" across the front, and gave an impassioned talk to my four-legged friends, about to take the Garden spotlight in quest of the Best-in-Show crown.

As I closed my resounding oration, I harkened back to their early days, when, as just puppies, they used to gnaw on shoes, or, in most cases, on old slippers. It was a sentimental moment. "Now you're going to go out on the famed Madison Square Garden floor seeking the most prestigious dog show award of all — this is the time to give it all you've got — just remember your early days as pups when that old chewed-up shoe meant so much to you. Well, this is your chance to WIN ONE FOR THE SLIPPER." The dogs were up for it, "asking for it" after my pup talk was completed.

One year I asked John Ashby, the official dog show photographer, to take my picture. I was aware of John's artistry in the show ring. "I'd be delighted," said John.

"Should I stand here?" I asked, taking a position away from the passers-by.

"Well, Bob, standing is not my thing. I'm a dog show photographer. How about jumping up on the table — on all fours, you know."

I got up on the table, on hands and knees, but could see Ashby wasn't satisfied.

"It's your expression, Bob," he said. "Let me try something." Ashby whipped out a piece of liver, designed to make dogs serene, but the odor gave me a look of nausea.

"Sorry, John, I don't like liver."

"Don't worry, I'll get the picture. Let's try squeaky."

John thrust out a toy animal emitting a piercing sound, but it left me recoiling.

It looked like my quest for a new picture was coming to an end.

But the project was saved. A good-looking woman sauntered by at this propitious moment, saw me down on all fours being photographed, and laughed uproariously at the sight.

She started me laughing too, and, at that precise moment, John Ashby snapped the picture.

"It's a winner," said Ashby. "Best-in-Show."

❖ ❖ ❖

Out of the mouths of babes come the most telling comments.

I had organized a "Miss Personality" contest at Westminster one year, and had handlers showing off a variety of appealing breeds, with a kids' panel I selected to serve as judges.

I interviewed each of my young selectors for about 30 seconds, and finally introduced my final judge, three-year-old Danny Clark.

Danny shuffled forward rather uneasily and made his statement on camera, "I gotta go potty." He was excused.

I wondered, as I turned Danny back to his mother, if Danny's honest declaration was also his critical review of this feature and its effect on him. He could have been right on target.

Chapter 35

I Also Remember

I've done thousands of broadcasts, thrilled to the artistry of the players, given vent to my emotions as I reported the ups and downs of the games, felt exhilarated by the roar of the crowd, and realized that, regardless of the outcome, I was the winner.

I was doing something I loved, I was at the mike, with the privilege of making my interpretation to the public — my calls, my words, my comments. It's still amazing to realize that I was paid to do this, and that what I've earned for my family has come about in such storybook fashion.

And yet I find it odd that I remember the players more than the games, except for those of particular significance, and I remember the off-beat occurrences most of all. The stories remain, long after the statistics are forgotten.

❖ ❖ ❖

DON CARNEY

Don Carney, sports producer at WPIX, which carried the Madison Square Garden events on TV in New York, gave me cigar-smoking lessons so I would look convincing smoking

Robert Burns cigars in on-camera commercials. "Don't stick it in the middle of your mouth like a lollipop. Look casual, side of your mouth. Practice holding the cigar so it becomes natural in your hand."

One night, after a Garden game, we went to a nearby restaurant so I could continue to perfect the smoking art before ordering a late night snack.

Between puffs, I put the cigar in an ashtray.

"What are you doing?" bellowed Carney.

"What do you mean, Don?"

"I mean, what are you doing with the cigar?"

"I'm putting it in the ashtray and then will put it back in my mouth. Anything wrong?"

"Bob, now listen to me. No self-respecting veteran, honest-to-goodness cigar smoker ever puts his cigar in an ashtray. That's only for cigarettes. The cigar becomes a fixture in your mouth right down to the nub. You can take it out when you eat or drink, but while just sitting here talking, cigar removal is a no-no. Get it?"

This was no kidding matter. I practiced hard so my career would not go up in smoke.

One break I got was when Dave Berman, a versatile Young and Rubicam producer, let me ad-lib the commercials, emphasizing the cigar's strong points. He wanted me to stress the long, even ash on their Cigarillos. My first attempt drew loud roars from our studio crew. Taking an admiring look at the cigar in my hand, I exclaimed, "Take a look at the ash on this cigar." I changed the words on my next attempt.

❖ ❖ ❖

BILL SHEEHAN

Bill Sheehan, a top advertising executive at Dancer-Fitzgerald and Sample, realized that, as a non-smoker, I seemed awkward trying to puff L & M cigarettes on camera. As they were an important sponsor on the Washington Senators telecasts, this called for a crisis meeting. Careers can hinge on what's decided. Fortunately, Bill had the solution.

"Bob, forget the smoking, but keep the package in the breast pocket of your suitcoat at all times with the sponsor's brand name exposed. Whenever you're on camera or in a picture, it will be seen. If you do that, we can forget the smoking."

I escaped again.

❖ ❖ ❖

THE GREAT FISH HUNT

One night, late in a ballgame at Griffith Stadium, the Senators were again plummeting toward the basement, when a frustrated fan threw something out of the second deck which landed near home plate.

I took a close look from my TV booth just behind home plate, and, by gosh, it was a fish. A dead fish. That fan from the stands had come closer to the plate than most of the Senators' pitchers that night.

This was late in the game. That meant the fish custodian had been sitting there a couple of hours holding a dead fish, stinking up the place.

Can you imagine this conversation with the person beside him?

"Excuse me, sir: Is that a dead fish I smell in your pocket?"

What was it like to sit next to this guy?

I promptly initiated a search for the unfortunate person or persons who had to endure this smell, next to the fish holder, and promised free tickets which I would personally purchase for another game. I figured such fandom should be rewarded.

We never did find the thrower or those around him. I always felt, though, that the thrower inflicted his own punishment by having to endure holding the fish all that time.

Oh yes, the fish was removed from the field, hopefully given a proper burial, and the game continued. Another memorable night of baseball, including a story with a hook, line, and stinker.

❖ ❖ ❖

EARLY WYNN

This Hall-of-Famer was an amazing athlete. Although he never tried it in the majors, he could pitch with either arm. Can you imagine the fun if he had confronted switch hitters with a little switch-pitching?

And Wynn could also hit from either side of the plate, providing a valuable pinch-hitting service to the Washington Senators with his batting ability.

One day, Wynn paid me a big compliment in front of my kids. "Your dad helped me get a raise with the Senators, and I'll always be grateful."

Wynn went on to relate how I had pitched to him every day while he sharpened his batting skills. "That's what did it," Wynn stated, "that got me a pay boost as a pinch hitter."

My kids looked at me as if I were Superman, and now couldn't wait until we got home. They brought out the bat and balls, threw me a glove, and said, "Okay, Dad, a little batting practice, please." That was an offer I couldn't refuse.

❖ ❖ ❖

ABE LEMONS

The 97-81 score when Abe Lemons' Oklahoma City team lost to Duke that afternoon at Madison Square Garden during a 1968 National Invitation Tournament game seemed almost incidental.

What I remember most is the halftime.

At the end of the first half, the OCU coach was furious. Normally a laid-back witty fellow with a distinctive drawl, he was in no mood for humor on this day. Lemons' team was being whomped, thrashed, and humiliated, and Lemons was so embarrassed when the halftime buzzer sounded he told them to forget going to the locker room. "You don't need rest — you haven't worked up a sweat — you need practice — and I mean a full-speed workout. You five are the skins, you five are the shirts — and I want to see some real old-fashioned work. I want these fans to know you guys can really play this game. Let's go."

They went at it. It was an all-out practice session at halftime — a sight I had never seen before or since. Drenched with sweat, they then began the second half.

Oklahoma City still lost the game, but it was the halftime I'll never forget. I don't think those players will, either.

❖ ❖ ❖

EDDIE MURRAY

When Eddie Murray joined the Mets a few years ago, I was

aware of his talent, but unaware of his reputation for being less than receptive to the press.

Not that it would have mattered much. I like to experience reactions first-hand.

With a cameraman, and holding a mike in one hand, I approached Murray in the Mets' locker room at Port St. Lucie during spring training. He was already in uniform, about 10 minutes away from taking the field.

"Hi, Eddie. I'm Bob Wolff. I'd like a few minutes of your time for a quick interview before you begin your workout. We can do it right here."

"Sorry, I can't do that."

"Why's that Eddie?"

"Because I have to stretch. I always stretch before I go outside to run."

"Sounds like a wise thing to do. Where do you stretch?"

"Right here on the floor. I just lie down and stretch all my muscles."

"Well, that sounds great. And I won't interfere with your stretching. I'll just lie down on the floor with you and we can talk while you stretch. I'll hold the mike so it won't interfere in any way."

I took off my coat, lay down on my back, and held the mike while asking questions, with the cameraman taping the proceedings.

The interview concluded, I got up, thanked Murray, and said, "You know Eddie, we ought to do this more often."

Murray smiled, perhaps more shocked than amused, but the mission was accomplished.

Was Murray tough to deal with?

Frankly, I still don't know.

But when it comes to an interview, I'll take it lying down.

❖ ❖ ❖

YINKA

I took a turn for the verse after hearing in 1994 that the Nets had signed their first-round draft pick, Yinka Daré of Nigeria, via George Washington University, to a reported five-year deal for nine million dollars.

OWED TO YINKA

Every team should have a Yinka...

That's a way to stop red inka...

Especially if he's a thinka...

And keeps away from those who drinka...

But if the coach feels need to tinka...

And the Yinka proves a stinka...

That's a million dollar clinka...

And Yinka Dinka will never do.

(My poetic license has not yet been renewed.)

❖ ❖ ❖

JERRY LUCAS

Jerry Lucas, a college and pro basketball whiz, practiced memory tricks that were unbelievable. For recreation, he'd memorize telephone books. Tell Jerry the name and he'd give you the number.

It's Not Who Won or Lost the Game—
It's How You Sold the Beer

When I called his games with the Knicks, including the
'72-'73 championship season, Jerry would say to me, "Leave all
your record books at home. If you're ever in need of information, get a message to me on the bench and I'll have the answer
for you. I have the pages memorized."

One day before appearing on a network television show,
Jerry met the audience members filling up a Broadway theater as they came in to watch the program. Jerry greeted
them all and asked their names and hometowns.

Later on stage, Jerry had a large group stand and Jerry
gave each person's name and town. An incredible performance.

On plane trips we had many discussions about memory
techniques. I memorized the old-fashioned way when I
learned players' numbers for games. No frills. Name and
number repeated until they popped out automatically, a condi-
tioned response.

Jerry used association — weaving stories in his mind
along with each number. Seemed more complicated to me, but
it certainly worked for him.

Jerry's mind was always active. One night after a game, I
gave him a ride to his home in Westchester County. He was
unusually quiet that night, and I asked him why. "I'm counting," he said.

"Counting what, Jerry?"

"The striations in the road. So far I'm past 2,000."

"You mean you're counting the cross bumps, Jerry. Is that
right?"

"That's correct."

"Well, I didn't mean to interrupt. Facts like that should be
accurate. Never can tell when they may be used. Beats counting sheep."

I dropped Jerry at his door. "What's the count, Jerry?"

"3,414" he said with a smile. "Remember that, it might help your next broadcast."

It never made the airwaves, but maybe Jerry will settle for a book.

Chapter 36

The Decision

Highlight tapes or records usually come from games of national significance, particularly if they're memorable individual performances or game-winning events.

In local game after game there also may be great plays, exciting moments, and clutch performances that bring the crowd to its feet, and the sportscaster's voice to a heightened level.

At the time, these are described as "unbelievable," "fantastic," "the greatest" and yet, as time goes by, they're supplemented by new players and new plays, and eventually become just memories. The words may remain the same, but without sufficient exposure and acclaim, the feats gradually become just boxscores of the past.

I've been fortunate to have been at the mike for many national highlights, but there have been many terrific experiences that remain only with me and the participants. They never had the glare of national spotlight and most were never filmed, taped, or recorded.

Some were just emotional moments, eventful because they involved feelings and compassion affecting players and fans alike, linked together in a sports drama.

Like the Herb Plews decision.

Herb, one of my Senator favorites, was a University of Illinois graduate. His high school at Helena, Montana, didn't field a baseball team, so Herb acquired experience playing American Legion ball and summer ball in the Butte Copper League.

His college team went to the finals of the NCAA tournament in 1948. The nifty infielder had already caught the scouts' attention with his .403 average which won the Big 10 batting championship.

Herb had come up with many memorable nights in the majors, including four doubles in one game against the Yankees' excellent pitcher, Bob Turley.

Herb was a team man, modest and dependable. He could play second, third, or shortstop, always with a top effort.

And on one sultry afternoon in Washington, DC, in a game that would have no national attention, Herb was involved in a personal emotional battle that touched me and the few thousand faithful who were spectators at Griffith Stadium.

Even the best of ballplayers have bad days as well as good ones. Often it's the result of the opposition. Occasionally, it just happens. That's the essence of the sport — the unexpected. There's a new script for every game.

On this day, the drama was built around Herb Plews. The Senators had built a sizeable early lead against Kansas City, and all they had to do was hold on for the win. That's when it happened.

Maybe it was the tides, the sonic boom, disruptions from outer space, or the vagaries of mankind, but on this fateful afternoon, steady Herbie who rarely erred was transformed inexplicably into "Mr. Futility." In one nightmare late inning, he attracted baseballs like a magnet, only they didn't stick to him.

They went through Herb, by him, off his wrist, and off his chest as runners romped around the bases and the Senators lead disappeared.

In the ninth inning with two outs, another Plews error and the Senators now trailed by one with men still on base.

Chuck Dressen, the manager, bolted out of the dugout. Would he keep Plews in the game, knowing that another blown opportunity would put the game out of sight?

And an even more burning question. Would he subject his third baseman to the humiliation of removing him from the game? Or would he consider that Plews' future might depend more on a vote of confidence?

Chuck went to the mound and motioned for Plews to join him. There wasn't a sound in the ballpark as the fans realized that a young man's career might be at stake. Would he recover from a benching if that were the Dressen choice?

I mentioned this on the airwaves. I could feel the tension in the ballpark. The human drama had now taken on more immediate significance than the ballgame.

Chuck Dressen was a peppery manager, an eternal optimist. Even after the most one-sided of losses, he'd say, "I saw some good things in the game. Just straighten out the pitcher's motion, get my clean-up hitter a little closer to the plate and we'll get them tomorrow." Of course, those tomorrow victories were infrequent, but Chuck always had a new plan in mind.

And his solution on this day brought about one of the heartiest roars of approval I had ever heard in the venerable ballpark. Dressen patted Plews on the back, gave a thumbs up sign to the pitcher, and trotted off the field to unrestrained applause.

Believe it or not, the next ball was hit to Plews. He bobbled it, picked it up, threw to first for the third out, and, after a collective sigh, the Senators came up for their last licks, behind by one.

It appeared that another Senator loss was in sight, but with two outs, Washington rallied. There were men on first and second — and with this drama now approaching the climactic moment — Herb Plews was coming up. The script had now come to its last page —failure or redemption ahead.

The pitch was on its way; Herb swung, and his scorching drive to deep right-center provided the sweetest sound of bat meeting ball I had heard all season.

My call was at fever pitch: "Base hit to right-center, rolling towards the wall. It's in there for extra bases. Here's the tying run coming across the plate — and now here comes the winning run — Plews has won the ballgame for the Senators! What a storybook ending! I'll never forget this ballgame." And I never have.

A rare sight took place after the game was over. Hardened ballplayers had tears in their eyes as they rushed up to congratulate Plews. They understood the inner feelings of going from despondency to elation.

Herb's wife, Shirley, clutching a handkerchief to her eyes, rushed up to hug her man, while Chuck Dressen took bows for staying with his guy when it counted. The locker room had all the emotion of a seventh game World Series victory.

The game is a vivid memory, although there was no particular baseball significance involved. It had no bearing on the pennant race or the season, or even on that day in the game's history. There is no film, no tapes, no recordings to preserve that game, nor are there many still living who may even remember it took place.

I share it with you, however, and it brings to mind so many emotional moments in sports that never live on because they didn't bask in the national spotlight, or have a record or championship at stake. These games are important, though, just as each day in our daily lives has meaning, regardless of the number of people who share it.

Herb Plews continued, after that day, stronger than ever in the field. Good ballplayers understand that lows and highs happen in sports, and the more disciplined ones take that in stride.

Our friendship with the Plews also continues. We all remember that game — and its happy ending.

Chapter 37

Concerned Millionaire

It was a sold-out night at the old Madison Square Garden, and tickets for this one had been gone weeks in advance. This was Harry Howell night, saluting one of the Rangers' all-time greats, with family and friends coming in from Canada, and former Ranger teammates being flown in by the Garden from all over the country to join in the tribute.

The event would have all the production of a big Broadway show. I had a handful of choice tickets reserved to entertain soccer club owners who were gathering in New York the day before as guests of the Garden. As president of the Garden's soccer team, the New York Skyliners, I was to serve as their soccer host. Soccer was a new venture for the Garden, in a short-lived league called the United Soccer Association. A club owner, Jack Kent Cooke, then with Los Angeles, had proposed that name, believing there would be promotional benefit in the abbreviated USA.

The owners were culled from bankrollers of basketball, hockey, or baseball teams in major league cities, and there were also some general managers in attendance as well. Judge Roy Hofheinz of Houston, Arthur Allyn of Chicago, and Gabe Paul of Cleveland were among the early arrivals.

The fervor for the new soccer league had been generated by the TV ratings of the World Cup, and by the crowd of 50,000 that Pele and Santos had drawn at Yankee Stadium playing Inter Milan.

The World Cup always commands great interest — it's nation against nation, the drama is fueled by nationalism and top-flight players. Pele, even in later years, drew huge crowds playing for the Cosmos. Santos and Inter Milan were clubs of world stature, well-known to large and appreciative Spanish and Italian audiences. Big names, powerful teams, and national pride were the drawing forces when these two foreign clubs collided.

These were vital ingredients in drawing spectators. The American entrepreneurs finally threw in the towel after realizing that poorer teams and lesser-known players would not lure fans in sufficient numbers to show a profit. The sport itself was drawing participants, particularly at youth levels, but converting them to paying spectators remained a problem. The sport is thriving in schools and in recreation leagues, but still trying for increased support on the pro scene.

Soccer moguls arrived for a scheduled afternoon Garden meeting the night before the Harry Howell game. A dinner and floor show had been planned for them that evening at a night club called "Downstairs at the Upstairs." Featured was a new brash woman comedienne named Joan Rivers.

After dinner and before the entertainment began, I told the assembled owners that, for those who wanted to stay over for the hockey event, they would be the guests of the Garden. "Just tell me if you want tickets and I'll have two good ones for each of you. I ask only one thing. Please don't take them unless you plan to use them — these are the hottest tickets in town. If you do take them and have to change your plans, please return them to the Garden box office so they can accommodate others. I'll be tied up emceeing the event, but the sales people will be there to help you. Of course, we hope you decide to go to the game."

Among those who asked for a couple of tickets was Lamar Hunt, the sports-minded young football owner who later would be involved with pro basketball, tennis, and other sports in addition to pro soccer. Lamar was a member of the fabulously wealthy Hunt family from Texas, but one would have never known from his appearance or manner. Soft-spoken, modestly dressed, this sports tycoon shunned the spotlight. Intelligent, down-to-earth, inconspicuous, and thrifty, he downplayed his wealth and power.

The day after the successful Harry Howell night, the box office manager called to congratulate me on its success, and relate an unusual story. He said, "Bob, there was an envelope left at the box office with a note saying, 'Please add this to tonight's gate receipts.' It was signed Lamar Hunt." The note went on to say that, at the last moment, he had to fly out of town. Knowing that you had told everyone that tickets were so much in demand, on the way to the airport, he had come by the crowded lobby, sold his tickets at the listed price, finally got to the window and left the money in the envelope for us. Pretty thoughtful, right?

I've thought so to this day. Lamar Hunt is a multi-millionaire who cares about the other guy.

Chapter 38

Storage Space

Sportscasters have to fly. The events don't come to them.

I usually found the skies friendly, but the ground rules sometimes caused problems. As a constant airline commuter racing from event to event, it was vital that this male got through — on time. This was particularly true on Eastern Airline commutes from Washington to New York where I sped directly from LaGuardia Airport to Madison Square Garden. For speed on overnight trips my zipper bag included my shaving kit, clothes, and broadcast material which I studied en route.

"I'm sorry but the bag won't fit under your seat. It will have to go in the storage compartment."

"But I need this bag with me to work on the plane, and I can prove to you it will fit."

"It looks too large."

"Just let me show you that it isn't. I have to study these notes for a broadcast. They're inside plus my overnight things. I plan to work on my numbers and notes during this plane trip, and then get off the plane in a hurry."

"Sorry, those are the rules."

"Look, I understand the rule and will go along with that. I'm just saying that when I get on the plane I'll show you there's no problem. In fact, I'll guarantee it. Just send an agent aboard with me, and I'll prove it."

"Your bag will be safe in the luggage compartment."

"Safety is not the problem. The problem is speed. I can't wait for the baggage to come off the plane. I have a race against time. Just let anyone you designate follow me to my seat and I'll show you this bag will fit under it. If it doesn't, the bag is yours to stow. This is a fair request."

"I know it can't be done, but we'll take a look."

A service agent tracked me to my seat. I opened the bag, and quickly deflated it. Pulling down overhead compartments, I put my shaving kit in one of them, my underwear in another and my shirts, ties, and socks in a third compartment.

I kept my broadcast material in my now shrunken bag for use after we took off. The bag fit easily under my seat without any question.

"See, no problem," I said to the agent. There was no need for him to answer. He just walked away, shaking his head.

When the plane landed, I quickly repacked my bag, sped off the plane, and was on my way to Madison Square Garden.

A little dramatic, but recommended as an emergency solution if the compartments aren't already filled.

Chapter 39

Brooklyn Bum

I've heard the saying "clothes make the man" and I guess it has a bit of validity. I wasn't thinking dress code, though, one hot afternoon when, as commissioner of the Atlantic Collegiate Baseball League, I spent the afternoon watching two of our teams in action. The ACBL is a summer league funded for many years by Major League Baseball to aid in the development of outstanding collegians rated as pro prospects.

The league, which has sent hundreds of young players into the pro ranks, and has garnered college athletic scholarships for many others, is staffed by baseball people whose remuneration is the inner reward of helping these youngsters get a showcase for their talents. A bonus is the enjoyment of watching top-flight baseball.

One Saturday afternoon I made the trip to Queens, New York, to watch our Long Island entry play against the Brooklyn-Queens Dodgers.

The playing field this day was located on the grounds of the Creedmoor Psychiatric Center, and, except for families, scouts, and some team and league followers, the rest of the spectators were patients, some of whom seemed occupied with their own agendas.

Before the game, I went into the Brooklyn dugout for a short visit with my son Rick, who was playing second base for the Dodgers. To ward off the hot sun, I had on my wide-brimmed African safari pith helmet. My ensemble included a faded Hawaiian print shirt, baggy pants, and a pair of old high-top black sneakers.

I guess, in retrospect, I seemed to fit in well with the others roaming around the grounds.

A teammate watched apprehensively as I approached Rick, shook his hand, and then sat beside him for a few minutes before leaving.

"Rick," the teammate said after I left, "you gotta watch yourself. Some of these people may be dangerous. You can't tell what they're thinking. Did that fellow identify himself?"

"Yes, he told me he was visiting today as the commissioner of the league."

Rick's teammate roared with laughter. "See what I mean, Rick. Commissioner, eh? That's a hot one. We've got to get a guard down here. That strange duck may come back. Next time he may tell you he's the president."

Rick felt it would be far better to spell out the facts. "I wouldn't worry about him. He's coming back after the game so we can visit some more. He's my father."

"Gosh, Rick, I'm sorry to hear that. Please forgive me. I didn't mean to kid about that. I hope you understand. This must be very difficult for you. Please forgive me."

Rick straightened him out later.

As for myself, I retired the black sneakers, decided a baseball cap would be more appropriate, discarded the old Hawaiian shirt, stayed with my creased pants, and decided that the commissioner should always look the part. Of course, it wasn't as comfortable.

Chapter 40

The Joy of Receiving

I've always believed there's more satisfaction in giving than receiving. Teaching has always appealed to me. So many of my sportscasting students at St. John's and Pace Universities and at Bill Raftery's summer sportscasting camp have gone on to productive careers. The talent is theirs, but I delight in having passed on a few suggestions that may have made their paths easier.

Sometimes, though, the roles are reversed. I became the receiver — in the most surprising ways.

Bruce Catania went to Scarsdale High School in Westchester County, New York, and took my summer sports journalism class at Pace University.

A few years after he graduated, he called me with this request: "Bob, I'm a producer now with Westinghouse Television, and am putting together an Olympic program called 'Manhattan Gold.' I need a host and narrator, and you're my choice. Will you do this for me?"

I was flattered by his phone call, and thrilled with the result. The program proved to be a cable ACE award winner.

One doesn't need awards, though, to have happy experiences. Some years back, I added soccer to the list of sports I have done on TV and radio, and served while the league lasted, as president of Madison Square Garden's professional soccer team. When the Cosmos and Pele triggered a later resurgence of interest in the sport, I received a call from Larry Jennings who was in charge of an extensive marketing campaign for the Tampa Bay Rowdies. The Rowdies had caught on big-time in Tampa, and Larry told me he'd like me to play a role in their TV and radio plans.

There were financial considerations, though. Larry wanted me to fly to Tampa from New York to consult one day a week, and also suggested that I might commute there to put together a Rowdies' weekly TV show.

A first-hand look convinced me that this operation was big-league in every way, with creative, enterprising people behind it. When they asked me if I would add play-by-play and half-time shows to the consultant work, I decided to rearrange my schedule to do so.

I did have one reservation. I was concerned that the Tampa sportscasters might feel as if I were intruding on their domain. I also realized that my commuting to Tampa might strain their TV-radio budget.

I was well received however, the ratings were high, and the columnists were kind. When I met the WTOG-TV station manager, Jim Dowdle, I expressed my appreciation for importing me from New York, particularly as I assumed he was not that well acquainted with my work.

"I know you very well, Bob," Jim said, "and that's why I thought you could help us. And you're doing just that."

"I'm flattered, Jim, but curious. When did you hear me?"

"Well, let me explain: When I graduated from Notre Dame,

I joined the Marine Corps and, as a first lieutenant, was stationed at Quantico, Virginia, in 1958 and heard you every day doing the Senators' games. I felt I had the voice and knowledge to be a sportscaster myself after I got out of the service, but I needed a few more tips as to how to begin. So I wrote six letters to six sportscasters I admired, and you responded.

"Not only did you answer, but it was a long typewritten letter outlining all the steps to take. I was so grateful that you had taken all that time to write that I put that letter in my personal file, hoping that, sometime in my life, I'd have a chance to thank you in person.

"That chance came here in Tampa. When the Rowdies told me they'd like to bring in Bob Wolff to work on the games, I said 'absolutely — go and get him.' It was a good decision."

I didn't remember my letter, but it was gratifying to hear that the time I took to answer mail could have a meaning in others' lives.

It was also exciting to find that Jim Dowdle went on to make his mark in the communications field — in fact, became one of the nation's top executives.

Throughout the years, the *Chicago Tribune* had become well aware of Jim's work. After adding to his laurels as general manager of the Tampa TV station, Jim Dowdle became president of Tribune Broadcasting. The Tribune Company acquired the Chicago Cubs in 1981. Jim was promoted to executive vice president of the Tribune Company, overseeing their broadcast and newspaper properties, and the Chicago Cubs. He doesn't need to be a sportscaster to get the best seat in the park. The entire ballclub is part of his domain.

A large part of the joy of receiving selection to the Broadcast Wing of the Baseball Hall of Fame is the outpouring of mail and phone calls, newspaper articles and TV and radio columns — all of which are treasured mementoes of my life.

Newsday put its congratulations in a flattering editorial, written by James Klurfeld, editor of the Editorial Pages. I wanted to write and thank him as I had the others who wrote to me or about me, but I didn't know whether to refer to him as "Dear James" or "Dear Jim."

I decided to call him in person instead of gambling on the salutation. When he answered, I said, "I just wanted you to know how much I appreciate what you've written, but wasn't sure whether you prefer to be 'James' or 'Jim' in a letter as we haven't formally met so I thought I'd call to express my thanks on the phone."

"Thanks for calling, Bob, but just to clear up the name matter, you used to call me 'Jim.'"

"I did? When did this happen? I just don't seem to remember."

"I didn't expect you to. It was in 1963 or '64. I was going to Syracuse and worked as a sportswriter for the *Daily Orange*. You were televising a Syracuse football game, and called Val Pinchbeck, then our sports information director, to provide a spotter. I was the man. It's been a long time since then, but I'm delighted that our paths have crossed again. My congratulations, Bob, your selection was well deserved."

It's fascinating to me the way that coincidences occur in life, but it adds to the zest of living, and it reinforces belief that there's meaning in every person involved in one's life — all having a role, large or small, which may not be apparent until some future time.

The unexpected makes every day an exciting adventure.

Chapter 41

Ted Williams

Even his teammates were in awe of Ted Williams. Certainly his opponents were. When Ted took batting practice, all other warm-up activity in the ballpark came to a standstill.

Players in both dugouts stood up on the top steps to watch the master in action.

Fans arrived early for this special treat. His drives were met by "oohs" and "ahs" of excited spectators who could now boast they saw Williams hit one.

To maintain a personal relationship with Williams, it was vital to understand his reactions.

The ultimate baseball perfectionist, if Ted didn't hit the ball well with his pre-game swings, I learned not to approach him until he had a protracted cooling-off period. He would stomp out of the batting cage if he failed to meet his personal standards, fuming, cursing, and running over anyone in his path as he strode back to the dugout.

To Ted, this was failure — even in batting practice. He had let himself down, and, in his mind, the situation was even worse because he was being watched by his baseball colleagues.

Ted would change completely if this happened. The same person who was smiling and chatting with me in such amiable fashion before the game would rush by me snarling as he tore through newsmen and poised cameras like a fullback crashing through the line.

After a 10- or 15-minute period, I would chance resuming my conversation with Ted, and, more times than most, the dark cloud would have disappeared, and his good mood would have returned.

No other player I've covered took batting practice as seriously, but, then again, when it came to baseball, every move counted with Williams. I understood his passion for perfection.

I had to deliver on television, though, and it was mandatory to have him on TV with me every season as a pre-game TV guest. This was my obligation to viewers, listeners, and sponsors.

I chatted with Ted on all his visits to Griffith Stadium. I suggested good restaurants in DC, told him I'd be pleased to give him a ride to any one of them after a game, suggested some sightseeing places he'd enjoy, and, in general, established a cordial friendship. I found him delightful company, and a good friend. Sometimes we just talked hitting, and it didn't take long to get him wound up dispensing his scientific theories.

One night my opening question was, "Ted, why do you like to take so many first pitches?" This triggered a fascinating soliloquy on the art of waiting for his pitch. The night before Ted had taken a called strike three. He ended this topic with a smile. "So I believe in studying the pitchers before I swing. Take two strikes if I have to. Of course, last night, I took one too many."

Ted was besieged by TV and radio interviewers whenever

he emerged from the dugout. I tried to avoid the impression that I was just another questioner in the electronic pack. I had learned this lesson early on one day when I was walking in Williams' direction before a game, holding a microphone in my hand. Williams, who was having a catch near his dugout, saw me approaching with the mike, scowled, muttered, and shaking his head to signify "no" looked as if he might relish wrapping the mike around my neck.

I kept walking right by him, and asked a player in the dugout to be my pre-game guest. But after I got off the air that night, I went to the Red Sox locker room for a chat with the master.

"Ted, there was no reason to get so upset. I was approaching you as a friend, just to say 'hello,' not to go on the air. I was carrying a mike, but not to interview you. That certainly was not the time for that.

"Look, let's solve this, once and for all. You tell me when we can do a TV interview each season. Let's shake hands on an agreement, and any other time I come by, it's just to greet you."

"Better explain that, 'bush.'" (Ted's term for most of his teammates.)

"Well, when you're back in town, tell me now what your batting average has to be or the number of homers you need to hit in order to go on. If you meet your standards, we do a show together. If you don't meet your figures, I'll be coming by just to chat with you, but will not ask you to do an interview. Naturally, I'll be rooting for you to succeed. That would help both of us. Will you go along with my plan?"

Ted smiled, said "sure" and we shook hands on what his average and homers would have to be on his next visit.

And finally the time had come. Ted would be visiting

Washington, and he had lived up to his commitment. His batting average and homers far exceeded our verbal contract, and I anticipated a great pre-game show with his guest appearance.

Then it happened. Ted Williams was in the headlines, but not with his bat. "Ted Spits at Fans!" screamed the Boston papers. Sports pages across the country, and many front pages, too, detailed this unsavory act, and wrote of the imposing $5,000 fine levied on him by his ballclub.

Williams' wrath at some jeering fans and a critical media had finally erupted in this derisive action. Ted had few defenders, the Red Sox front office was furious, and the prideful slugger let it be known that he wouldn't discuss this in any way with the media — press, TV, or radio.

That included me. The Red Sox were coming to town, and Ted and I had a verbal contract, but with the press embargo, would Ted live up to his promise?

The spitting episode came about in August 1956. In the 11th inning of a scoreless game against the Yankees, Williams misplayed a flyball and the booing increased. To end the inning, he had made a difficult catch, but seething with rage, as Ted came toward the dugout he had looked up at the Fenway press box, thumbing his nose in a gesture of defiance and then spit toward occupants of the ground-level boxseats, a double salute to media and fans.

And now here he was at Griffith Stadium, having lived up to our statistical early agreement to go on. I approached him immediately — no time for wariness.

"Ted, I find this difficult to say to you but, please understand, it's my job. Earlier this season you promised me if you had the batting average we agreed upon and the homers you needed by August, that you would go on my pre-game show. I told you I wouldn't bother you otherwise, and here you are with all conditions met.

"A promise is a promise, but, as a friend, I'm going to let you out of our agreement if you feel you can't handle it. You see, Ted, to do my job, just as you do yours, I have to ask you about your actions in Boston, and your feelings towards the fans and the media. If you want to back out, I'll understand. I just want you to know what I have to do.

"It's your choice, Ted. I hope the answer is 'yes,' but our friendship will continue if you say 'no.'"

There was a pause. Williams looked at me, then past me at the practicing players, then turned back. "What time's the show, Bob?"

"7:45, Ted."

"I'll be there — and Bob, ask anything you want."

The interview took place near the Senators' dugout. After exchanging a few pleasantries with Ted, I hit him with the big question relating to his spitting display in Boston. "Ted, would you explain your feelings and reactions to the press and the fans?"

Ted's whole being took on an immediate change. His eyes narrowed, his body became taut, he clenched his teeth, and he looked down at the ground where the spikes of his right foot seemed to be raking imaginary pebbles. Then he raised his head and started to answer.

At that precise moment, a fan came bounding over the low wall onto the playing field and approached us. I had the sinking feeling that this long-sought interview would be a disaster — that the mood would disappear — that time would run out.

As the fan came within a few feet, intent on saying "hello"

or joining our conversation, I kept smiling and said, "Pardon me, sir, we're doing a broadcast. Come back and see me later."

The fan persisted. "Oh, is that Ted Williams? Are you on camera now?" I kept smiling and pumped my arm vigorously to wave him away.

"I didn't mean to interrupt," the fan came back to make an apology. I turned back to Williams and tried to regain the mood. Out of the corner of my eye, I saw the fan finally moving back towards the seats.

By this time, I felt the bottom might have dropped out of the interview. There could be no starting over. This was being filmed, game time was approaching, my allotted time was nearing an end, and Williams might not be accessible again. Editing could not change the intrusion.

"Ted," I began again, "explain your reaction to the press and the fans. Do you feel you owe them anything?"

"My reaction to the press, Bob, is that they should cover the game honestly, write what they see, not what they think. There are certain writers who can be vicious. They deal in personalities and opinions and sometimes when they don't like something they may pinpoint an individual who is not responsible for a situation. That's what irritates me the most — untruths written about me in the papers. That makes me so mad I explode at times — and do things I wish I hadn't done."

Ted looked out toward the field where coach Billy Jurges was hitting grounders to the infielders. "Many players have devoted their lives to baseball. The press and fans should realize that and appreciate their contributions.

"I admire ballplayers. They don't have to be the great sluggers. There's Willie Miranda — and Clint Courtney — and Kaline and Kuenn — and Mantle, of course — we all know we owe something to the fans. Without fans there wouldn't be baseball. But how about what those players bring to the game? Fans owe something to them too.

"I'm sure that over 90 percent of the fans are for me. I get irritated at myself, too, for an error or a boot but I give my best, and that's all I can do."

Time was running out. I turned to Ted and suggested laughingly that we consider our personal contract for his next TV appearance with me. Ted interrupted. "Bob, I've known you for quite a while, and I just want to thank you for being so fair with me. That's why I went on the program with you."

I thanked Ted and the program ended.

There's a postscript. A few weeks later I took this Ted Williams film, added a previous interview I had done with Mickey Mantle, and put a "Dugout Chatter Show" together as a pilot for a syndicated television series. I felt confident about its possibilities.

I flew to New York and showed the pilot to Lev Pope, the general manager of WPIX, New York and to a potential sponsor, the Colgate-Palmolive Company. My hunch was correct. The show was bought as the New York Yankees' pre-game program beginning the following season, and other markets followed.

It was exciting to get the go-ahead competing against major film companies for important airtime. It also meant days and nights of hectic activity for my small staff to come up with a full slate of shows.

My hardy group — assistant Maury Povich, cameraman Lou Prawde, secretary and project manager Jackie Lower Dunn, and Byron's Film Lab in Washington, were equal to the challenge. More teams signed up and we were off and running.

There's an added twist to the story. When I showed the

pilot film in New York, the fan's unexpected interruption was included. I had been concerned about the reaction. As it developed this intrusion became a memorable part of the show. While I was trying to maintain a smiling composure, the camera focused on Ted's face. The stark contrast between my smiles and his grimaces provoked gales of laughter. Ted's face contorted, his eyes narrowed, and his anger mounted while the fan persisted. Ted's aroused reaction was readily apparent. More important, it was understood.

Of course, this syndicated breakthrough might never have happened if the Splendid Splinter had not lived up to his promise to appear with me. It was a tough spot but Ted came through in the clutch.

Ted's emotional approach always seemed to me one of the reasons for his success. It seemed to trigger his energy in his zeal for perfection.

I always had great expectations for our interviews. The great expectoration proved to be an unexpected bonus.

Chapter 42

Patterns of Behavior

I'm not superstitious, of course. Come to think of it, do you know anybody who admits to believing in any of that stuff?

On the other hand, if something works, why change it? Could be worth repeating. Maybe the meal you had put you in just the right frame of mind to succeed. Or perhaps the path you took to the ballpark helped to clear your mind. Or the trinket in your pocket gave you a livelier step. Not that I'll admit that reliance on these unrelated items has any bearing on victory. In fact, the whole idea is preposterous. It is, isn't it?

Of course, there are patterns of behavior. For some unfathomable reason, they seem to work. Sometimes wearing the same clothes, eating the same meal, or repeating the same habits that worked well yesterday can bring the same success today. No guarantee, of course, but why risk otherwise? Admit it, they could have a bearing. Right?

Pens work. The same pen that filled out yesterday's scorecard with a victory should have enough ink in it for a few more wins before being retired. Lose one of those pens and the entire pattern of behavior can become totally disrupted.

During the 1995 season, I met a kindred spirit in Bill

Pulsipher, the Mets' pitcher. I was doing the TV play-by-play of some Mets' games, and, while chatting with Pulsipher, noticed the nine pairs of spikes in his locker.

"I stay with a winning pair of shoes until it lets me down," Pulsipher confided to me.

"If it doesn't do well, I use another pair the next game.

"I've got my starting shoe rotation pretty well set, but they all get a chance with me."

"Suppose you lose a game, Bill. It could happen, you know. What happens to those losing shoes?"

"They get another chance. I speak to them. I take them out of rotation, let them cool off. When I think they're ready to try again, I lace them up, give them a little pep talk, and figured they've learned by experience. Some respond very well."

"You're not superstitious, are you Bill?"

"Those aren't real superstitions — they're just er — er."

"Patterns of behavior?"

"Yeah, that's it — that's just what they are."

I have proof positive that these amazing coincidences actually work. When my son Bob was pitching for Princeton, I knew for a fact that, on the last leg of my long car trip to the campus, there was a sequence of 15 timed lights along Route 1 from New Brunswick to Princeton. If all the lights turned green before we approached them, the victory would be guaranteed.

It took timing, of course. The drive had to be at just the right speed so there'd be no stopping. Occasionally, one had to slow down to about five miles an hour to make sure the red light would turn green, but that was just a minor inconvenience. Make all the green lights, and all Bob had to do was take the mound.

The only time the streak was in jeopardy was when my

wife said to me, "Darling, we have all the lights with us today — just two more to go, and we'll make them all."

I recoiled in shock. Everyone knows how words spoken before the fact can jinx everything. I was in agony. This unexpected declaration was tantamount to shouting, "He's got a no-hitter with two outs to go." You know what happens.

I gripped my lucky pencils, pens, coins, ink eraser, and all the victory-insured charms in my pocket to ward off the problems about to arise — they'd have to come through for me now — or this long trip could end in disaster.

We got by the next light barely — one to go — and it turned red as we were approaching. "Jane," I shouted, "slow down to a crawl. We got to make this last light. Barely move — one or two miles per hour — just idle along. Just don't stop — just creep —we can't stop."

The seconds were ticking away. We were close to the light — still red — inching closer and closer — just a few feet away now. I crossed my fingers, crossed my legs — yelled "turn" and the game was saved. The green came on in all its magnificent glory. I felt limp — victory was now insured upon our arrival — and knowing the result in advance, I could enjoy Bob's winning all the more.

Of course, there was a little more work to be done. Before every pitch, standing behind the home plate screen, I bent over to pick up a twig or stone. If what I held in my hand worked for a strike or an out I'd hold on to it. If not, I'd discard it and do some more ground-scavenging. I held on to the better sticks and pebbles — the ones that seemed to be real winners, and at the end of each inning put them in my pocket for use in the clutch —for this game or future ones.

Visitors to my home today can view this ancient rock garden still on display in one of my bureau drawers. I've held those twigs and stones to this day.

But believe me, I'm not superstitious. I don't believe in that. Bret Saberhagen is, though. He also believes in the number nine. Bret has nine T-shirts in his locker, and changes his shirt after every inning. Tells me it's because he sweats a lot. A pattern of behavior, of course. And Bret makes sure not to stray too far from his beloved number eight which he wore as a kid. When he was traded to the Mets and eight was taken, he settled for 18, but when 18 didn't live up to expectations, he decided to try number 17, figuring that adding "1" and "7" would add up to his school number "8" again.

But don't tell Bret he's superstitious. He's just as normal as you and me.

Before I close this chapter, I have to make a confession. My son Bob didn't need any of my idiosyncrasies to make himself an excellent pitcher. He manufactured his own good luck. I've never watched any pitcher, pro or amateur, who got more out of his potential. Bob realized that deception, coupled with superb control, could win games and he mastered both.

Aware that he'd never have great velocity, Bob concentrated on setting up batters by working inside and out, and mixing up sliders, screwballs, forkballs, and curves without falling behind in the count. He'd go three or four games in a row without issuing a walk.

A standout in high school, he became a pitching ace on his championship American Legion team where he also batted in the third spot as a self-made switch hitter. At Princeton, he was undefeated in the New York Metropolitan area, defeating St. John's three times, Seton Hall twice, NYU, Fordham, Army, and others.

Well known on the mound for his hesitation pitch and his "junk ball" style, Bob always felt he had the game in hand when opposing batters, drooling, started to line up at the bat rack, waiting to get their licks. He knew they'd be overswinging victims. "It was embarrassing, though," he confided to a reporter, "when my catcher Arnie Holtberg kept throwing the ball back faster to me than I pitched it to him."

One of the great delights of my life was discussing pitching strategies with Bob and noting how he worked towards his "out pitch" as carefully as a scientist in a laboratory.

He always knew how to win, and his teammates, somehow, always played their best defense behind him. They realized he thrived on groundball outs, wouldn't walk anybody, and kept the pace fast. They also knew errors wouldn't faze him, nor would men on base.

Bob delighted in his college success, and enjoyed his relationship with his coach, Eddie Donovan. His focus remained on amateur ball, however, and his coming career which was to be medicine.

Occasionally, we might mention professional ball as there were always scouts at his games, but Bob was realistic about his major league chances. "Dad, I've been fortunate to win at every level and against some of the best college teams in the country, but no matter how well I pitch I'm never going to beat the clock on those radar guns. I'm a winning pitcher, but there seems to be more interest these days in hard throwers. Instead of playing summer ball after my junior year, I'm going to take Organic Chemistry at Columbia University, a course I'll need for medical school."

At graduation, Bob received the award for outstanding achievement in pediatrics at Boston University School of

Medicine. Watching him pitch, I led the cheers, but when his medical honor was announced at the graduation ceremony, I led in tears of joy. Bob continues to be a winner now at helping others.

Dr. Robert Wolff, an outstanding pediatric neurologist, has now switched from baseball to tennis. How fitting that he was an award winner in the Baseball Hall of Fame tennis tournament the day before my induction.

Chapter 43

Batting Leader

One night I was speaking at an umpires' banquet in New Jersey.

I like umpires. I remember Don Adams' umpire routine addressing the umpires' graduating class at training school. "Some of you will continue to achieve. You'll go on to even bigger things, to greater heights, using your vision, your judgment and your authority. We'll be proud of you. Now the rest of you will remain umpires...." He always got a laugh. Maybe it's the way I tell it.

When the dinner was over I called my TV station, News 12, Long Island, to check for any messages. Patrick Waldron, the sports producer, told me that while he was back in the edit room, he had overheard a Chicago telecast in which the announcer had said, "Rick Wolff is the best prospect on the field."

"Can that be Rick, your son?" Pat asked. "What's he doing in Chicago?"

It didn't make sense, but the news was intriguing. Same name — a ballplayer — and then the light dawned. Rick had told me he was writing a story for *Sports Illustrated* about what it would be like to revisit the minor leagues, and would be traveling to South Bend, Indiana, to chronicle the White Sox farm team there — while in uniform, if possible.

"Pat, you say, the telecast was coming from Chicago, and Rick was apparently starring in the game?"

"That's right. It was on a Chicago station. I heard them talking about Rick but didn't have time to spend checking it further."

That was the clue, though. I called Chicago and found out that SportsChannel, Chicago, televised the White Sox games, but as this was an off night for the Sox, they had focused their camera on the Sox farm team to show Chicagoans how the youngsters were being groomed, only to discover it was an old-ster who was making the headlines.

There'd be one more game in the series the next night, and nothing could make me miss it. I bowed out of all shows and engagements, booked an early morning flight via Chicago to South Bend, and was there to watch the concluding act of this unbelievable baseball drama.

Following Bob and Rick around the countryside is no new experience for Jane and myself. Watching Fathers' League, jayvee ball, high school, American Legion, college, Cape Cod League, Atlantic Collegiate Baseball League, and the New Rochelle Robins has been our way of life. If there were games Jane and I couldn't attend, our daughter Margy, an excellent athlete herself, was a knowledgeable emissary. A former bat girl at her brothers' games, she could describe the fine points of play with the jargon of any big-league broadcaster, and had a journalistic sense of the key points. If she hadn't gone on to a degree in nursing, her animation would have served her well as a sportscaster.

Rick had added new adventures as a Detroit farmhand in Anderson, South Carolina, and Clinton, Iowa.

What happened in South Bend, Indiana, unfolded like a fantasy script. I'll let Rick tell the story as he wrote it on assignment for *Sports Illustrated*, and return with post-game comments.

RICK WOLFF'S TALE

Fifteen years ago I played my last season of professional baseball for the Clinton (Iowa) Pilots. It was a Detroit farm team, but Clinton has since become part of the San Francisco organization. It has been renamed the Giants, but it is still in the Class A Midwest League. I've undergone some changes too. Now I'm 38, and I'm an editor who leads the domesticated life of a New York suburbanite — wife, two children (now three), station wagon. But this June I got a chance to go back to the Midwest League to play in a few games as a minor leaguer again and to report on just how life in the cornfields of baseball has changed over the years since I admitted that sliders are awfully tough to hit and that at 24, I was getting too old to play a kids' game.

Within 24 hours after I left Manhattan and found myself trying to squeeze into a pair of double-knit game pants in South Bend, Indiana — home of the Class A South Bend White Sox of the Midwest League — something happened. Something that I cannot account for, something that should never have happened, something that could only happen on a ballfield in the middle of America.

WEDNESDAY EVENING. Stanley Coveleski Stadium is located in downtown South Bend. You go down Main, make a right on Western, and you can't miss it. In a town with only a couple of multistory buildings, the stadium light standards are a major feature of the skyline. The ballpark is right across the street from Union Station and the rail yard, right next to the old Studebaker plant.

Rick Patterson, the field manager of the White Sox, greeted me, gave me the once-over and told me straight out with his Southern baseball twang, "Don't worry, Rick. We're going to treat you just like any other ballplayer here. That's what you want, isn't it?"

"You bet."

"Then go with Scott [Johnson, the trainer] and get suited up. And stick around for tonight's game. Who knows? We may need you."

"Well, skipper, to tell you the truth," I found myself saying, "I thought that maybe I'd just work out a bit tonight and then shower and go back to the hotel. It's been a long travel day, you know." I winced as soon as I said the words.

"Yeah, sure," Patterson said, "whatever you want."

I went along with Johnson to find a uniform big enough to fit my expanded waistline and a cap small enough to protect the scant hair left on my head. Along the way, I got a real good look at "the Cove." First off, understand that the Midwest League ballparks I played in had wooden stands, usually with a peeling coat of green paint and always with as many splinters as your derriere could handle. The clubhouses were cramped quarters equipped with nails on which to hang your clothes, and the showers — which were always clogged — never had a thought of hot water.

But the Cove, just a year old, was minor league heaven. Each player had a personal stall in the big clubhouse. The trainer's room was equally big and complete with all the latest gizmos of medical technology. And there was a weight and training room full of equipment. Then there was the manager's office. Did I mention that the entire place was carpeted? Now, out these doors you can take the elevator to the general manager's office. Elevator? In Class A? I asked one of my new teammates if all the ballparks in the Midwest League were like the Cove. He smirked and said, "Are you kidding?"

A few minutes later, the deed had been done. I looked in the full-length mirror in the clubhouse, and the mild-mannered editor from New York had been transformed into an official member of the South Bend White Sox. Yeah, the double-knit pants were a bit tight, and the low-cut stirrups weren't exactly my style. But there was no mistaking it — I looked like a ballplayer. After 15 years I was back on the roster.

The pregame workout went fine. At the start of the evening's game with the Burlington (Iowa) Braves, I sat back on the dugout bench (aluminum) and watched the Sox take a 7-0 lead behind 21-year-old lefthander Freddy Dabney. In fact, Dabney was coasting along with a no-hitter into the sixth inning when he accidently clipped a Braves batter, who then promptly charged the mound.

Within seconds I found myself in the midst of a nasty brawl that left one Burlington player flat on his back with a bad cut on his nose and another with his knee crunched. Dabney had suffered a broken finger on his nonpitching hand, and to add to the indignity, he was one of several players given the heave-ho for having had a major role in the fight. So much for Dabney's no-hitter.

Back on the bench I felt a stirring of pride to have been one of the first of the White Sox to join in the fray. Not that I threw any punches, but I was on the field, holding back bodies, trying to reestablish a sense of order. I mean, it's been a long time since we had a bench-clearer at one of our editorial meetings. I was chuckling to myself when Patterson yelled down at me in the bottom of the eighth, "Wolff, grab a bat — you're up next."

The last thing I wanted to do tonight was pinch-hit. Especially in a game where feelings were red-hot. After all, it was now getting chilly; my arms and legs ached a bit. Then there was the matter of not having seen a minor league fastball, curveball or slider up close and personal in more than a decade. And I had *never* seen a split-finger fastball from the batter's box.

But the skipper had issued an order. So I grabbed a helmet and a bat. A wooden bat, a genuine Louisville Slugger. I tried to remember how to swab it with the pine-tar rag.

By the eighth inning, the game was well in hand, and nobody in the stands seemed to pay much attention to the "new kid" coming to bat. And quite frankly, there wasn't much to report. The 22-year-old Burlington righthander fed me a steady diet of blurry fastballs and hard sliders that seemed to break off at right angles. All I dreamed of doing was making contact, and that's all I did. With a 2-2 count, I lunged at a slider and tapped a weak roller out to short. I lumbered down to first, where I was an easy out, and then found myself heading out to the field for the ninth.

The first two visiting batters fanned, and the final man up hit a routine, powder-puff grounder to me. I picked it up cleanly, whisked it over to first, and then, to my surprise, found myself engulfed by my teammates. From their perspective, it was something just short of miraculous for this fossil to have hit a dribbler to short and fielded a grounder. As we went up the runway to the clubhouse, I pulled one of the Sox coaches, Kirk Champion, off to the side and asked about the team's reaction to my play.

"Look, Rick, it's like this. The consensus is that you're definitely going to hurt us as a team," Champion said with a straight face. "The real question is, how badly will you hurt yourself?"

THURSDAY EVENING. At game time, the temperature was 49 degrees with a sharp breeze out of the north. I took infield practice, checked the lineup card, and found my name penciled in for the ninth slot. I actually felt pretty good; I even had the first play of the night come my way at second, which I again handled.

Burlington was starting a lefty, and, as my teammates returned from the plate, I quizzed each one on what the pitcher was throwing. "Aw, he's just throwing pus," third baseman Greg Roth angrily said. "Nothing but pus." That reassuring thought began to point up evidence that perhaps minor league ball hadn't changed all that much. All batters, no matter what the era, always claim that the opposing pitcher is throwing nothing more than pus — even if the pus happens to cross the plate at 90 MPH plus.

I came to bat to lead off the bottom of the third. By now, the crowd of more than 5,000 (the Chicken was in town for the evening) began to take note of the old-timer. I fouled off a couple of pitches down the rightfield line and then — with an 0-2 count — laced a clean, solid, line-drive hit into right center. Nobody was more surprised than I was. What I remember more than anything else was that glorious feeling of hitting a pitch right on the money with a wooden bat, that true feeling of a bat conquering a pitch.

In the fifth inning it happened again — another shot to right. In the sixth, I hit a one-hopper to short, but on my fourth time up, in the eighth inning, I lofted the ball to right for a sacrifice fly and my first RBI in the Midwest League in 15 years. In the field, I was making the plays, picking up grounders, catching pop-ups, taking care of business. I was charged with one error. That occurred when a pickoff throw from the pitcher literally went through my glove; the ball broke one of the strings between the fingers. Remember — I had been using that glove before most of my teammates had been born.

Late in the game, I began to notice a change in my teammates; Wayne Busby, our hyperkinetic shortstop from Mississippi said, "Hey, old-timer you better keep your cap on, 'cause people are going to start thinking there are two Golden Domes here in South Bend." And from one of the pitchers, "Tell us Rick, you must have known him, what kind of player *was* Babe Ruth?" I had become the target of some old-fashioned needling —the ultimate acceptance in baseball. Even the Latin American kids got involved. I caught Clemente Alavarez, our talented catcher, pointing at me and saying to infielder Leo Tejada, "*Mucho loco, si?*"

It was a glorious, wonderful evening, and I was even awarded the game ball by Patterson, who laughed and shook his head in disbelief. And, of course, the White Sox had won again, 4-1. I showered and looked around for a celebratory beer.

"Sorry, old man, but no beer in the clubhouse," I was told. "Organizational policy."

No beer? After a win? Things have changed a bit. Sometimes, I guess, it's for the better.

FRIDAY EVENING. A crowd of 3,000 curious fans came out, all eager to see whether the oldest player in South Bend

Sox history could somehow keep the magic going. I hadn't slept much the previous evening; even an ample dose of Extra-Strength Tylenol couldn't keep my throbbing legs from demanding that I come to my senses and return to the safe confines of suburbia.

But game-time came at dusk and Patterson even moved me up to eighth in the order. When I walked on four straight pitches on my first at bat, I could hear the manager of the Burlington club, Jim Saul, screaming at his befuddled young pitcher, "C'mon, just throw strikes to this old geezer. He can't touch you! He can't even see you!"

I next came to bat in the fourth inning with a teammate on second and first base open. The Braves pitched to me instead of intentionally walking me, which made me furious. I hit a scorcher. The first baseman was able to snare it in the air, and then he fired to second to double up the runner. O.K., it was an out, but it was yet another solid shot right on the sweet part of the bat. In the seventh, the Braves started a reverse shift with everybody shaded heavily toward right on me. Again feeling my oats, I pulled a liner down the third base line for a base hit.

Finally, in the eighth, I came to bat with men on second and third. "Geez, you've gotten your hits, your RBI, your walks," squeaked Busby. "You might as well go for it all and try to smack one over the Pepsi sign." Nice thought, but even fantasy has its limits. Yet on the first pitch, I swung, made contact and saw the ball headed for extra-base land in right centerfield. Out of the corner of my eye, I saw the ball bounce on one hop against the wall, and I cruised into second with a stand-up double and two more RBI. It was at this point that I realized the fans were on their feet, giving me an ovation and cheering my name. Even the Burlington shortstop came over to me and asked, "No offense, mister, but how the hell are you doing this?"

Patterson sent in a pinch runner, and I came off the field with both arms in a triumphant Kirk Gibson-style salute. Amid a sea of high fives and happy congratulations from my teammates, Patterson started laughing and gave me a big bear hug of approval on the dugout steps. "Old man," he chortled, "you just did what every old ballplayer has dreamed of doing. To come back one more time and do it again. By golly, you did it!"

And that was that. Over the three days, the Sox had won three, and I finished 4 for 7, with three RBI, one BB, one SF, one E and a league-leading .571 BA. The next morning, under sober grey skies, I headed back to New York and to my seat on the 7:59 train. The South Bend White Sox climbed on a bus and headed for a three-game series in Kenosha, Wis.

But for a brief moment, I had been able to go back and experience minor league ball again: The unique smell of fresh pine tar. The grainy grip of a wooden bat. The sound of spikes clacking on a cement runway. That final pre-game rush of adrenaline as you stand at attention during the national anthem. The playful but biting wit of teammates. And, of course, the pure joy of hitting a pitch solidly for a base hit.

Jim Bouton, another ballplayer who knows something about comebacks, once wrote that "you spend a good piece of your life gripping a baseball and in the end it turns out that it was the other way around all the time."

❖ ❖ ❖

It was an unbelievable ending. After Rick completed the

rounds of post-game interview shows and reporters' questions, he returned to the locker room where a celebration was underway.

Rick had performed his own Hollywood script. In the exhilarating afterglow, after hugs and congratulations, I kiddingly suggested to Rick, there'd be no need to try an encore. The locker room scene looked like the seventh game win of a World Series. From somewhere came a bottle of champagne. Rick was mobbed by his teammates, and manager Rick Patterson, in a stirring speech, told his troops how proud he was that Rick could be with them for a few days and become part of the team.

After more toasts and cheers the mayor of South Bend came rushing into the locker room to present Rick with the key to the city. What a celebration! It was staggering.

Could there be more?

Yes, there was. Rick emerged as the unofficial batting leader of the Midwest League, and, after South Bend won the championship, Rick was invited by the team to come back for the ceremonies, and, at the presentation, receive a championship ring.

Sports Illustrated told Rick, "Forget about writing about minor league life. Just give us a story about yourself." That's what Rick handed in — the diary which you've seen — and *SI* headlined it "Triumphant Return" (Aug. 21, 1989).

National TV followed. "60 Minutes" put it on their drawing board, but finally yielded when they couldn't assemble enough game video except for the second game that was beamed back to Chicago. But ESPN on its "Major League Baseball Magazine" sent a crew out to follow up on reaction to Rick's story and came up with an exciting coast-to-coast feature. It was an amazing experience and a climactic chapter to Rick's athletic successes, which I had witnessed from grade school to Harvard and then in the pros.

Chapter 44

The Crowning Moment

And now it was about to happen. I was in Cooperstown, standing before a sun-drenched crowd estimated at 30,000, stretching back over acres and acres of land. Seated behind me was a spectacular gathering of baseball's all-time greats, returning Hall-of-Famers, along with the new inductees, and family representatives of deceased new members.

One can plan a sightseeing trip to Cooperstown, but there's no way to chart the routes, the detours, the highways, the roads, the turns, the stops, the goes, that kept me on the path for inclusion in the Broadcast Wing of the Baseball Hall of Fame, the sport's highest honor.

Nor can I enumerate or thank properly all those whose work and talent and guidance and friendship kept me moving in the right direction. I share the joy of this thrilling once-in-a-lifetime experience with them as well as with the viewers and listeners who have always made me welcome as part of their electronic family. My family and I are most grateful.

Hall-of-Famer Ralph Kiner was at the podium to introduce me — the lead-off inductee. The moment had arrived.

Chapter 45

At the
Cooperstown Podium

I'm not used to seeing crowds like this.

I broadcast in Washington.

There are over 200 buses here from Philadelphia. Two cars started out from Washington — one broke down.

Of course, there were a few big occasions. The presidential opener, for example. That was always significant. If the Senators won that game, they'd be in first place. Unfortunately, they had to play the rest of the season.

But winning or losing didn't concern me when I made my debut as Washington's first telecaster in 1946. I was in my twenties, had made it to the big leagues, and life couldn't be sweeter. Few thought that television would amount to anything. Fortunately, the man who hired me — Les Arries, Sr. — did. There were only two TV stations in the country — Washington and New York on the DuMont Network, and about 200 sets in Washington. I didn't have one, but the audience was swelled by my wife, Jane, who, on occasion, would take a bus from our small apartment to the TV station to watch my flickering image. In New York, my parents could go to Gimbel's basement, and watch me on this new invention. I take no credit for television's later boom.

I had ample opportunity to learn though. I discovered that while voice, and style, and technique were important assets, preparation and content are the keys to survival. And there's something else that all of my distinguished Hall-of-Fame broadcast colleagues have in common — wearing well — game after game, year after year.

I also learned that the way to a sponsor's heart was by selling his product. In those pioneer days, I was also the commercial spokesman, and, as I rarely smoked or drank, I was uniquely unqualified for that job. There were no filmed commercials in those days, there was no tape — just me — live.

I was given cigar-smoking lessons, cigarette-smoking lessons and spent a month in spring training learning how to pour beer correctly — with either hand — the first switch pourer in the majors.

Of course, broadcasting the games was a daily delight. The Senators had some great players including Hall-of-Famers and league leaders. Unfortunately, they just didn't have enough of them on any one team. They played well, but remarkably the other clubs played a little better.

Clark Griffth and later Calvin had no other business to sustain them. Their business was baseball. They had to rely more on ingenuity than money. As did early TV.

I called a lot of records with the Senators — set against them — like Mickey Mantle's longest homers. We always kept a tape measure handy. Of course, Washington had some great sluggers, too, like Harmon Killebrew. And Jim Lemon and Roy Sievers who were members of my singing Senators group

— a very harmonious team. I played the ukulele — and there were Mickey Vernon, Pete Runnels, and countless more.

Getting to Washington was another great break in my incredible good fortunes. I had taken my .583 high school batting average and my well-worn centerfielder's glove to Duke University intent on making the majors.

I broke my ankle in a rundown play and was invited to sit in as a guest on the local CBS-WDNC broadcasts of the games. When the regular broadcaster left, I was offered his job, so that broken ankle was a big break in every sense of the word. I told my coach Jack Coombs that I had this job offer, but my ambition was still to get to the majors — and asked the coach what to do. "Bob," he said, "if you want to get to the majors — just keep talking."

More study time proved another good break and a valuable lesson. It proved to me that success was possible with a little inspiration, but a great deal of perspiration. My sportscasting career has been based on that principal — preparation.

After Duke, I was commissioned as a Navy Supply Corps officer and sent to the Harvard Business School for training before going to Camp Peary, Virginia, to go overseas with the Sea Bees. And talk about great breaks, at Camp Peary I met Jane Louise Hoy, a beautiful Navy nurse. That was the greatest break of all. But I was on my way to an advanced base in the Solomons. Would Jane wait for me — and would I return? Jane said she'd wait, and I returned in what I considered miraculous fashion.

Overseas, I discovered that the Harvard training was excellent for shipboard routine, but didn't apply to the mud and rain problems of advanced base supply. I wrote a book with before and after pictures explaining how the Navy regulations and procedures relating to advance bases should be revised and sent the book off to the Navy Supply Department.

Within two weeks, there were airmail orders to fly back immediately to Washington. I reported to Commander Hugh Haynsworth, received a letter of commendation, and was assigned to rewrite the Navy Advance Base supply regulations and training books. That's how I got to Washington. Jane and I were married at the Bethesda Naval Chapel, and here in Cooperstown are celebrating 50 great years together.

While still in Navy uniform in Washington, I began broadcasting sports on the *Washington Post* radio station and worked with an excellent journalism model, their news director and my long-time friend Bill Gold. Then I added TV to my schedule with DuMont TV. A few years later Paul Jonas, the Mutual Sports Director, signed me for his football Game-of-the-Week and then came network TV assignments on NBC, CBS, and ABC. In 1954 I also began a wonderful 36 years working Madison Square Garden events.

My schedule was bountiful, but I had one big ambition to fulfill — broadcasting the World Series.

In 1956 the All-Star Game was played in Washington and the sponsor, Gillette, used me to represent the host city. I guess they liked my work as they asked me to broadcast the '56 World Series too, and I had the great fortune to be at the mike for the Don Larsen no-hitter. In the booth with me was Gillette's talented producer, a fine gentleman and long-time friend Joel Nixon, who is here today.

That World Series propelled me into two more Series assignments, and then I joined Hall-of-Famer Joe Garagiola on the NBC-TV "Game-of-the-Week." What a thrill that was. I've also had the pleasure of broadcasting with Hall-of-Famers' Jack Brickhouse, Chuck Thompson, and Lindsey Nelson and have heard and admired all those in the Hall.

For the past nine years I've been the sports anchor at News-12 Long Island, and have done baseball sports specials and play-by-play for SportsChannel, New York. That's been delightful.

To make this journey even more complete, our family is with us today, including our son Bob, a former crafty pitching star at Princeton, our son Rick, an excellent second baseman who played on a Harvard World Series team and later in the Detroit organization, and our daughter Margy, a superb athlete herself and the original bat girl for her brothers.

With Bob's wife, Susan, Rick's wife Patti, and Margy's husband Tom Clark, are our All-Star team of the future — nine grandchildren. Our All-Star nine.

The poet — Rolfe Humphries — wrote: "The crowd and the players are the same age always, but the man in the crowd is older every season."

I've been a man in the crowd for many years — and the joy is always there. The sights and sounds of baseball, the strategies, the ups and downs, the talk, the kidding, the roar of the crowd —the pleasure is constant — regardless of time.

Baseball gives adults a chance to relive their youth — on or off the field.

Kids, not burdened by adulthood, don't seek a Bill of Rights. Kids don't have need for associations, agents, lawyers, committees, or representatives. They depend on adults to provide opportunities to play the game, watch the game, and afford the game. It's the obligations of adults to make this happen. It's accomplished best by grown-ups who still remain young at heart.

At the Hall of Fame's first induction ceremonies, Babe Ruth reminded spectators that kids are the backbone of the game. Babe, they still are.

I have been so fortunate — in my life — in my career. My wish is that I've been able to contribute the same happiness to the lives of others that they've brought to mine.

I've had the good fortune to be at the mike and make the play-by-play calls at some of sport's most memorable moments.

But the call that's the greatest in my life was the call made by Ed Stack, the chairman of the Baseball Hall of Fame with the historic news that I had been selected for the Broadcast Wing of the Baseball Hall of Fame. That's the greatest call of all.

What does receiving this Hall of Fame honor mean to me? In one sentence — I feel as if I've gone to Heaven — before I died.

❖ ❖ ❖

Before leaving the podium, I grabbed my ancient battered ukulele, and lived a fantasy by strumming and singing before an understanding baseball crowd that knew I was doing so with joy in my heart. Baseball is fun to me and always will be.

It was gratifying to note the response to my song — and the spirit in which it was delivered.

The Associated Press wrote, "After giving his acceptance speech, Wolff highlighted the already-bright 90-degree day by picking up a ukulele and playing 'Take Me Out to the Ball Game.'"

I prize and treasure the columns that were written, the letters, congratulatory cards, telegrams, and mementoes that were sent. It was an emotional and moving experience that can come only once-in-a-lifetime but remains in baseball's treasured history. I had the privilege of sharing it with my wife, our family, our friends, and fellow fans, and that wonderful glow continues.